German Colonization Past and Future

German Colonization Past and Future

The Truth About the German Colonies

Dr. Heinrich Schnee

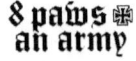

The Scriptorium

First published in 1926: Dr. Heinrich Schnee, *German Colonization Past and Future: The Truth About the German Colonies,* London: George Allen & Unwin, 1926.

Reprint: Copyright ©2022 by The Scriptorium
wintersonnenwende.com
versandbuchhandelscriptorium.com

Our cover design is based on Rudolf Hellgrewe's 1911 [est.] painting of German settlers in the Namib Desert of German South-West Africa.

Print edition ISBN 978-1-7781445-8-5
ebook ISBN 978-1-7781445-9-2

All rights reserved. No part of this book may be reproduced in any manner whatsoever without written permission except in the case of brief quotations embodied in critical articles and reviews.

CONTENTS

1. Introduction — 1
2. Biographical Note: Dr. Schnee — 40
3. How the German Colonies Were Seized — 43
4. The Myth of German "Colonial Guilt" — 58
5. The Alleged Militarism in the German Colonies — 73
6. The Allied Powers and Their "Sacred Trust" — 96
7. The Treatment of the Natives — 105
8. The Question of Slavery and Forced Labour — 139
9. German Rule and Mandate Rule Compared — 159
10. What the Natives Really Want — 182
11. The Future - the Way of Peace — 192
12. Notes — 198

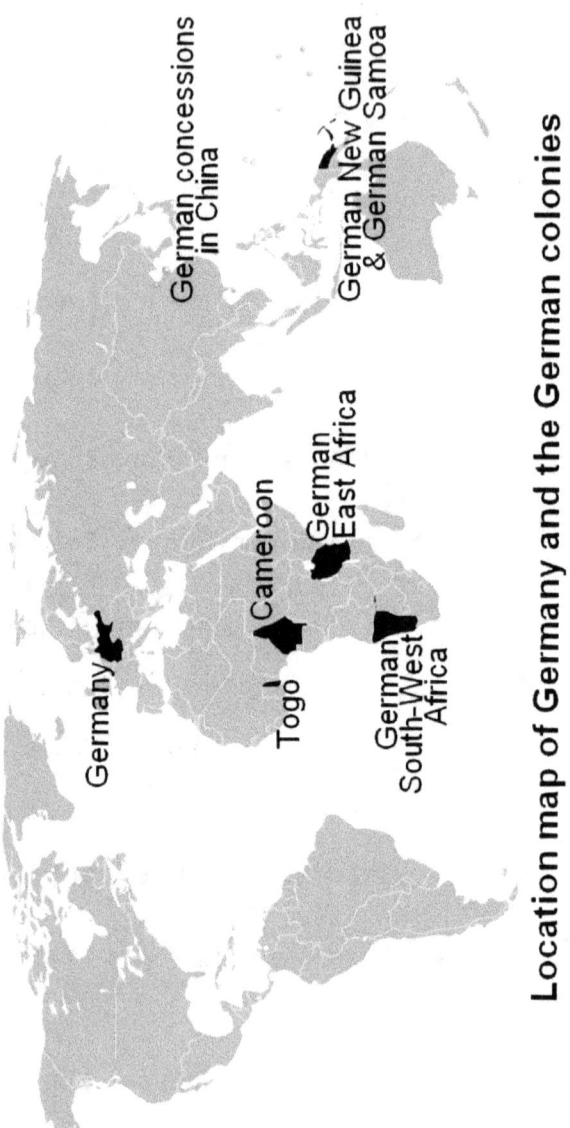

Map labeled and added by The Scriptorium.
Map source: the "New World Encyclopedia", newworldencyclopedia.org

1

Introduction

In the third chapter of *The Four Georges,* Thackeray, that valiant crusader against hypocrisies and shams, strikes vigorously at the practice of bearing false witness in time of war. Referring to the struggle with France under the First Napoleon, he says:

> "There was no lie we would not believe; no charge of crime which our furious prejudice would not credit. I thought at one time of making a collection of the lies which the French had written against us and we had published against them during the war: it would be a strange memorial of popular falsehood."

Mr. Baldwin, who, for the good of his countrymen, continues to administer to them one excellent moral tonic after another, each after a judicious interval, spoke to much the same effect in his late very noteworthy address to the students of Edinburgh University (November 6th), an utterance in pleasing contrast to another rectorial address to youth spoken in Scotland a twelvemonth or more before. "With war and the preparation for war," he said, "go the stratagems of diplomacy, the dropping of the code of morals, *a holiday for truth,* and an aftermath of cynicism.... In the arena of international rivalry and conflict men have placed patriotism above truthfulness as the indispensable virtue of statesmen."

Time, which changes most things, does not appear to have lessened the proclivity to mendacity of patriots of the baser order, nor yet the gullibility of the unreflective mass of mankind. Much of the propagandism evoked by the Great War amply proves this. All the leading belligerent nations suffered from calumny and misrepresentation manifold, yet it is probably safe to say that they usually gave as good or as bad as they received.

The book which I have been invited to introduce to the English-speaking public deals with one phase of that propagandism. Though now to us little more than a memory, its evil effects live after it, and the worst of these is that it has created a perplexing colonial problem which cannot by any possibility remain as it stands to-day. Accordingly, it is the purpose of the following narrative to show wherein Germany's reputation and success as a colonial Power have been unjustly called in question, and to give reasons why the return to her of colonies is an act both of duty and of necessity.

Of the author the short biography which follows says all that should be needful to convince fair-minded and just-thinking readers that they are dealing with one who speaks with authority and whose reputation as a colonial administrator is above reproach. A man with such a record deserves both credence and a respectful hearing. Moreover, Dr. Schnee has written with moderation as well as knowledge, wisely remembering that this is a question which cannot be helped forward by violence of thought and language. Bitterness, passion, blindness, and folly did the wrong, and an unbiassed and unselfish respect for truth, justice, and right, with a clearsighted recognition of the dangers inseparable from the political situation which that wrong has created, will alone clear the way for full international understanding, so helping powerfully towards the fulfilment of Europe's urgent need of a pacified and a pacific Germany.

The service asked of me I perform with the greater readiness since during the war I exerted myself to the utmost to combat the spirit of revenge - not for the sake of the Central Powers, but for our own sake and that of a world which had been bidden to look forward to a better future - and in that spirit to reinforce the view, held by so many high-minded fellow-countrymen, that our nation should, territorially, emerge with clean because empty hands from a struggle to which the Government of the day committed it with fervid protestations of pure motive and unselfish purpose. Let us criticize some of the methods of the "old diplomacy" as we may, it had at least established, and that long ago, the wholesome tradition of renouncing territorial advantage in the event of international disputes and the resulting conferences. There were many excellent precedents of the kind for their guidance and encouragement had the Allied Powers been concerned to adhere to their earliest declared war aims.[1] Sound policy and national interest pointed equally to the wisdom of such an attitude, since the annexationist policy, which all too soon found favour in influential quarters, was bound to breed endless mischief and to provide fuel for further conflagrations.

Unhappily, it was the lower and unworthier choice that was eventually made in 1919. By that time the hands of all the Allied Governments were fast bound by secret agreements of which the world only heard when it was too late for effective protest. "Peoples and provinces are not to be bartered about from sovereignty to sovereignty as if they were mere chattels and pawns in a game. Peoples may now be dominated and governed only by their own consent." So said President Wilson on April 2, 1917. Yet never before in history was there such a wholesale "bartering about" of human flesh and blood - not all, but in large part, no less senseless than callous - as that which took place in Paris two years later.

So it came about that all the efforts of far-thinking men and women to secure a peace of moderation, uninfluenced by bitterness and passion, were so much vain beating of the air; for let it be confessed, in fairness to the blind leaders of the blind of those days, that a majority of the nation, whether consciously or from apathy, willed it so. It is related of Bishop Butler that, walking one night in the garden behind his palace, he "suddenly turned to a chaplain and amazed him by the question whether public bodies might not go mad like individuals, for in truth nothing else could account for most of the transactions in history."[2] The Treaty of Versailles and the national attitudes which it rejected at the time it was drawn up may well form a monumental illustration of Butler's theory.

If on merely technical grounds I were challenged to justify my association with this book, I might point to two facts - the first, that I have frequently discussed both the good and the bad sides of the German colonial movement in books and other writings during the last thirty or more years; the second, that I prepared, by request, the handbook on "German Colonization" which was published by the British Foreign Office, as one of a large series, for the information of the members of the Paris Peace Conference.

The author of this book has a strong case, and he has made the most of it. This vindication was inevitable. Those who were our antagonists in the late war and suffered from misrepresentations which they hold to have been both ungenerous and unjust, have a perfect right to ask us, now that the atmosphere is clearer and serener, to weigh more calmly and scrupulously the many accusations offered for our consumption in the heat and passion of strife, and to compare them with the actual facts. Not less is it our duty, if we value the old reputation of our nation for veracity, fairness, and justice, to give to such answers as this careful, patient, and even indulgent consideration.

It is, perhaps, true that most men and women are weary of war controversies, and wish nothing more ardently than to forget them. But honesty and decency require of all of us that in such a matter we should do as we would be done by. I put the question to any Englishman of probity, jealous for the reputation of our own imperial heritage and our fitness to continue its custodians: what would be his attitude towards indiscriminate attacks made on British colonial administration by German or any other accusers? Would he accept misrepresentation in silence and indifference, or rebut it with vigour and appeal from fiction to fact, from false witness to verity? This is what Dr. Schnee claims the right and the obligation to do, and at the end of his narrative he draws the consequences.

While accepting a general responsibility for this book, as having in some sort "edited" it, I must not be identified with every statement and phrase. The narrative came before me as a translation based upon, yet not in all points identical with, a German original, published several years ago. I have not felt it my duty to compare the text of the two versions, since Dr. Schnee, being responsible for both, was clearly entitled to vary the later text at his discretion, but I have nevertheless been at pains to verify practically all quotations and other references cited, and at my request Dr. Schnee has also furnished me with the evidence or original text, as the case might be, upon which some of his more arresting assertions are founded.

Let me say at once and quite frankly that while I do not suggest, nor does the author of this book, that all the indictments of German colonial administration which were circulated in this and other countries as part of a singularly "intensive" war propagandism were wholly baseless, I do maintain, as he does, that these indictments were a mixture of the false and the true, that they contained much culpable misrepresentation, and that the impression which they produced, and were designed to produce, on the public mind was wholly unjustified. Particularly do I endorse to the full his contention that the motives which at a later date were officially pleaded in support of the appropriation of Germany's colonies were not moral and disinterested, as the world at large was told and possibly believed at the time, but political and egoistic. Hardly anywhere, outside the countries which have benefited by the annexationist policy pursued in 1919, is a different opinion any longer held.

Dr. Schnee has a good deal to say about the failure of the Allied Governments and their representatives in Paris to honour the conditions for Germany's surrender which were laid down in President Wilson's Fourteen Points of January 8, 1918, and then in the Five Points contained in his Speech to Congress of September 27, 1918, and formally endorsed by the Allied Powers; but a few supplementary words on that subject may not be out of place. It is worthy of note, as indicating the attitude of the saner section of public opinion at that time, that a few days after the date last named (October 2, 1918) the Washington correspondent of *The Times* quoted from the *New York Evening Post* (a journal known to be then in close relations with the White House) the reminder that in all his utterances the President had "eschewed anything that might lead the German nation to think that he contemplated... a peace which would contravene its legitimate economic aspirations"; and addressing his remarks to British readers the correspondent urged that it should be made "clear once for all that we do not propose permanently to penalize a regenerated German nation for the crimes of its present overlords." A little later *The Times, in propriâ personâ,* reprinted both the original "Fourteen Points" and the subsequent "Five Points" in full, as though assuming that these pronouncements would govern the peace settlement.

Unhappily for Europe and the world, the Fourteen Points and the Five were ignored. Wilson said in his Speech to the Senate on January 22, 1917, that the coming treaties and agreements should embody terms that would create a peace that would be "just and sure and worth guaranteeing and preserving," that would leave behind it no humiliations and no galling memories, and "not merely a peace that will serve the several interests and immediate aims of the nations engaged." The better way was known, the worse was chosen. Wilson's failure two years later to induce his colleagues in Paris to adhere to the pledges given to Germany, with his own resulting abandonment of them, is one of the most lamentable facts about the Peace Conference, and it is certain that much of the disillusionment, unsettlement, and despondency which have since settled on Europe has flowed from this source. His capitulation to the unsympathetic influences which surrounded him can only be explained by one or both of two reasons - **(a)** the consciousness that in seeking an idealistic settlement he stood alone and had no hope of carrying through his avowed policy of "impartial good will," and **(b)** his eagerness to rescue from the threatened wreck of his hopes his favourite design of a League of Nations.

Even the latter he failed to secure in the form in which he had envisaged it. "That partnership," he said on December 4, 1917, "must be a partnership of peoples, not a mere partnership of Governments." Yet after the event his friend and coadjutor Robert Lansing wrote: "Whatever it may be called, or however it may be disguised, it is an alliance of the five great military Powers."[3] This malign character is changing, and will doubtless disappear increasingly as time passes and the Governments of the minor States cultivate courage and independence; but the League, as at present constituted, continues in form and effect to be still far too much what President Wilson said it ought not to be.

In the determination of his ultimate attitude towards the future administration of the German colonies it is probable that President Wilson accepted at their face value all the accusations against German administration which had been assiduously circulated by official and other propagandists, just as he similarly accepted other misleading statements, emanating from French and Polish sources, which he had no means of verifying.[4]

At the same time, it is conceivable that Wilson, who, like most forward-looking idealists, was apt to see what he wished to see, discerned in the Mandate idea later and larger possibilities, and conceived of it as the nucleus of an arrangement for placing all the undeveloped territories of the habitable earth, with their native populations, in the care of a great International Trust, so releasing them from the arbitrary rule of many conflicting States. For to the last he believed that "a great wind of moral force was moving through the world," and continued under the spell of his noble vision of "just men everywhere coming together for a common object." It may be that an International Trust will be the final solution of the problem of native territories and their exploited peoples. It is certain that the framers of the confiscatory provisions of the Treaty of Versailles have converted to that view many thoughtful people who never before gave to it sympathetic consideration. And why not? Why should so large a slice of the earth's surface be "owned " by a few privileged States, and in how many cases do these States hold their territories by titles which would, in the view of an impartial international tribunal, carry either legal or moral sanction?

Dr. Schnee makes a forcible answer to the indiscriminate charges which have been advanced by partisan advocates not merely against individual German officials and traders guilty of misdemeanour - for that would have been legitimate - but against Germany and the entire German nation. Apart altogether from their exaggerations and suppressions of fact, examples of which are plentifully given in the following pages, two important and essential considerations were culpably ignored by the authors of these charges. One is the fact that at the time that grave abuses and wrongs admittedly occurred in some of her colonies Germany was in the stage of learning and experiment, having no living colonial tradition behind her and still laboriously endeavouring to create and train the corps of officials necessary for the administration of vast native territories. In the circumstances mistakes, failures, misconduct, even crimes, were inevitable. But was the early era of any colonial empire - even our own - free from abuses? Is any colonial empire entirely free from them to-day ? No allowance whatever was made for the difficulties inseparable from new tasks and utter lack of experience.

But, further, at that time and later Germany was under a militaristic form of government, and it was to this evil and its consequences, and not to any indifference on the part either of Legislature or nation, that the early "colonial scandals" were chiefly due. One of the British official publications issued with a view to defending the appropriation of Germany's colonies names a book of mine in evidence of administrative abuses. But in the book in question,[5] while reciting individual instances of the ill-treatment of natives, I certainly did not generalize, and I took care to make it clear that the German nation and its Parliament had at all times shown serious concern for the well-being of the native populations, and visited with disapproval and condemnation any administrative or other shortcomings which were brought to light in the colonies, herein setting an example which certain other colonizing nations, which need not be named, might have imitated with great advantage. In particular I paid a well-deserved tribute to the fine spirit of humanitarianism invariably shown by the powerful Centre and Social-Democratic Parties. I repeat that the root-evil at the time to which the "colonial scandals" referred was the fact that the colonies were too much left to military administration and a hard type of officialism. Great Britain's success as a colonial Power has been due largely to her practice of governing as little as possible; where the Germans failed, it was mainly through governing too much. That fault, however, had been recognized and was being remedied long before the outbreak of the Great War. Yet, so far as my knowledge goes, in none of the anti-German and pro-annexation literature, with a single exception, whether that literature was written to official order or emanated from private individuals, was to be found any recognition of the facts here stated, though in bare honesty it was due.[6]

Referring to the general national attitude to the colonies in Germany, I wrote in an edition of the book cited above published early in 1919:

> "With the reorganization of the colonial service and the cleansing of the administration, a humaner spirit has entered into the relationships between the officials and the native populations. Much has also been done for the development of the natural resources of the African colonies by the building of railways, and other measures. In these ways, and by the training of the natives to regular habits of industry, by the establishment of experimental farms, schools, hospitals, and the introduction of improved sanitation, etc., the material and moral welfare of the subject populations has been promoted.... Above all, the colonial movement has been re-established in national esteem and confidence. One by one the parties which originally either opposed it or held towards it an attitude of suspicion and indifference have come into line upon the main principle, that colonies are indispensable

to Germany's future, as an outlet for population, as a source of raw materials, and a market for the product of her ever-expanding industries. There is no longer in the colonial movement any trace of the old almost childlike credulity, but its place has been taken by a disposition to treat the colonies seriously, and on the whole by a greater readiness to recognize the moral obligations which empire carries with it. Thirty years ago the Germans played with their colonies as with toys; to-day their attitude towards them is that of sober men."

These words were written months before the decision to expropriate Germany was taken, and in recalling them I would add that the fact that so much parliamentary and national concern for the welfare of the colonies and their populations was exhibited even under the system of government associated with the last of the German war-lords gives ample warrant for the confident belief that to-day, when the German nation, for the first time in its history, is in effective control of national policy and affairs, these territories and peoples would count, under the care of their earlier and rightful trustees, on just, clement, and sympathetic treatment. The efficiency of German colonial administration in such matters as material development, sanitation, medical service, education and agricultural and industrial training calls for no defence, since in tropical countries the energy, enterprise, and success of the Germans in these spheres have nowhere been surpassed and seldom equalled. Indeed, Germany had not been ten years in occupation of her colonies before the British Foreign Office (1894) published a report by one of its officers stating that the development of the territories presented "a picture which must arrest the attention of the most careless observer, as showing what can be done by indomitable perseverance and patience with materials and in regions not always of the most promising description."[7] The year before Sir J. S. Keltie had written of East Africa:

"The rapidity with which the Germans have established themselves in the country and the wonderful progress already achieved have made a deep impression upon the natives - Africans, Arabs, and Indians alike - who contrast what the Germans have done in five years with the little accomplished by the English during the fifty years they were supreme at Zanzibar, forgetting that the position of the latter in the Sultan's dominions was very different from that of the former."[8]

Dr. Schnee has passed detailed and searching criticism upon the substance of the "colonial scandal" accusations and the methods employed in constructing the indictment. His presentment of this aspect of Germany's case may be left to speak for itself. I will only say in relation to the well-known Official Blue Book on German administration in South-West Africa - a production discredited by no less capable a critic than the present Prime Minister of the Union of South Africa - that no one capable of judging the value of evidence will give much credence to lurid stories based merely on native testimony. It is notorious that even amongst civilized peoples imagination, when tricked by memory, distorted by fear, or spurred by malice, often plays havoc with fact. The war yielded countless examples of the kind in all countries. Who does not remember, for example, the horrible "true story" of the gouging out of prisoners' eyes in Belgian hospitals which our Foreign Office had the manliness to probe and nail to the counter as false? Only within the last few days the ghoulish *Kadaver* slander against the Germans has been repudiated, and that handsomely, by our Foreign Secretary as baseless in the House of Commons. Let me recall a recent experience of my own. In the course of travels in South Africa during the winter of 1923-4, I was told of an unmentionable act of mutilation alleged to have been perpetrated upon a British soldier by Germans in the South-West campaign. Slow of belief, I became doubly so when a little later precisely the same story was told to me in another part of the country, though this time the cruelty had been perpetrated by Boers upon a fellow-Boer who had fought on the British side. Naturally, I now regarded the tale as only another proof that rumour is apt to be "a lying jade."

The Powers which divided between them Germany's colonies professed to do so in the name of morality, and subsequently they formally undertook to administer these territories "as a sacred trust of civilization." Governments and nations which claim to be more righteous than their neighbours set themselves a high standard of conduct, and it is not always one possible of attainment. In meeting the rash and dangerous claim that annexation was called for by ethical and humanitarian considerations, Dr. Schnee has struck back, as he was justified in doing. It is well for the best of us to be compelled at times to see ourselves as others see us. Those people who can patiently and approvingly accept allegations made against another country, whether ignorantly, maliciously, or even truthfully, yet are unwilling to listen to and impartially examine authenticated accusations made against their own land, have much to learn about the ethics of controversy and of conduct. Honest men and women, who want to know the truth, and to know it not partially and through glass of their own colouring, but wholly and clearly, will not resent the reminders contained in this book that, be the palliations as they may, many of the regrettable abuses alleged against the Germans under the older system of administration have occurred in our own oversea territories, and that some have not been eradicated even in the present day.

It must be allowed that in making his counter-charges against Germany's accusers - for France, Belgium, and Portugal have more to answer for than we - the author has exercised in general a commendable restraint, in strong contrast with the spirit of the publications which he is rebutting; though here allowance should rightly be made for the fact that the conditions and atmosphere of 1925 are happily different from those of the years of war. Nevertheless, there is in his indictment much that must make British readers, jealous for their country's honour and credit, feel uncomfortable, and perhaps resentful that attempts should have been made after the event to justify the forcible seizure of Germany's colonies by the claim of a moral superiority.

Enough has been said, however, about Dr. Schnee's presentation of the case for German colonization. In writing these prefatory words I am specially concerned to put forward considerations which in my view make the return to Germany of colonies - which and where is a matter of secondary moment - a matter both of honour and of policy for our own country. That some of the territories could not have been returned in any circumstances, and that she could not have been allowed to re-enter at once into custody of any of them, was, perhaps, a foregone conclusion, though Dr. Schnee may differ from me here. None the less, I believe that a great mistake was made in closing to Germany the door of Africa in particular with so unceremonious and demonstrative a bang, and hold that it would have been wiser, looking to the future, to have given her the hope of resuming her place in that spacious continent at a later date, perhaps on well-considered conditions of tenure and trusteeship, which might have applied to all colonial Powers alike.

And, first, the annexation of German territory was a distinct breach of the pledge given to our nation and the world at the beginning of the war. On the eve of the outbreak of hostilities we as a people, in common with our Allies, professed that the war was one only against aggression and domination, and the Prime Minister of the day formally repudiated all intent or thought of annexation, as did his leading colleagues later. That pledge the nation, in a noble mood of moral elation, gladly received and implicitly believed. Yet the struggle had not lasted many months before the Allied Governments were drawing up secret agreements for the appropriation of vast territories in three continents!

In the later formal partition of Germany's colonies in particular, Great Britain, to use an inelegant phrase, "did herself well" - far too well for her permanent comfort and health. Those, however, who believe that our Allies are as satisfied as ourselves with arrangements so greatly to our apparent present advantage should ponder carefully the comments upon the subject which still appear from time to time in the

French, Italian, and even the American Press. If our friends criticize us so freely now, what may be expected when the memories of the late military comradeship begin to fade and new men come upon the political scene to whom the ties and obligations of the present hour make no overpowering appeal?

When foreign critics talk of the German colonies they often speak as though Great Britain alone had taken them, so drawing a distinction which, though we may regard it as neither flattering nor fair, carries its own significance. The question who was primarily responsible for this defection from high principle - whether France or we - is one of little consequence. The fact that matters is that the thing was done, and that the avowals and assurances of disinterested aims which had fired the early enthusiasm of the nations were thrown to the winds. What made the annexations the more indefensible, and even indecorous, was the fact that almost without a single exception Germany's colonies were no man's land before she occupied them; not one was the result of conquest in the way that most colonial empires were founded. Far from invading the rights of other white nations, her title to these territories was confirmed by formal treaties, mostly with Great Britain, who received valuable equivalents, but also with France, Spain (here it was a money transaction), Belgium, Portugal, and America. At the close of a war one of whose most solemnly avowed purposes was to re-establish the sanctity of international law and agreements, it is not comforting to be told that it is permissible to ignore territorial treaties which stand in the way of assumed national interest. That doctrine used to be imputed only to the extremer advocates of Pan-Germanism and to German militarists of the Bernhardi school.

Later the annexationist policy had to be defended and given some sort of cloke of decency, and how moral pretexts were invented for the purpose is shown in this book. It is a pitiable story which no Englishman should be able to read without feelings of humiliation. The hollowness and insincerity of the plea that Germany had proved her incapacity and unfitness to bear the responsibility of governing native populations are best proved by the fact that never before had such incapacity and unfitness been suggested, for the testimonies, official and private, were all the other way; insomuch that at the very outbreak of the war our Government was negotiating treaties under which further territories - even British - would have passed under German rule.

For myself, jealous for the good English name, I shall never cease to regard these territorial gains as sordid and ill-gotten, and their seizure as the most ungenerous act ever perpetrated in the name of the British Crown, Government, and people. If our Allies were determined to despoil Germany in the hour of her weakness, our representatives should have let them do it and take the risks alone. Their first duty to England was to honour her pledge and keep her hands clean. The right course and the just course, I hold now as before, was to have acted towards Germany on the colonial question as we acted towards Belgium when the Congo excesses forced the Powers to active intervention. In neither case was the nation, as such, responsible for the misdeeds done in its name. The cure for the misgovernment of the Belgian Congo was the transfer of that region to the administrative competence of the nation. Germany, likewise, should have been given the opportunity of proving, in the changed political conditions, her capacity for just government, at first under mandate, with the promise that, on such proof being forthcoming, she should again take her place in the world as an independent colonial Power.

Referring again lately to war books which have been banished to the top shelves, it was interesting to find that this view, which I advocated from the beginning of the war, had a later spokesman in that well-informed writer, Mr. Edwyn Bevan. In his introduction to a translation of Emil Zimmermann's book, *The German Empire of Central Africa* (1918), he writes:

> "Supposing the political developments of the future should bring, let us say, the Social-Democratic Party to power in Germany, the question of German rule over black people would at

once become a very different one.... The whole question of a German oversea empire would take on a very different complexion if the German State came to be directed by a new spirit. It would probably not be safe to count on such a spirit as durable until a certain period of time had elapsed after the end of the war."

Accordingly he proceeds to suggest a provisional occupation, as I had done before. Had that course been followed, Germany in all probability would have been again in custody of some of her territories, and much heart-burning and resentment and the certainty of future trouble would have been spared.

But, further, the seizure of the German colonies is condemned not less from the standpoint both of national and international policy and interest. Men and women who are keen and cautious enough in the regulation of their private affairs are often strangely indifferent to the effects of acts done on their behalf in the domain of politics. Our statesmen, however, know well enough, though few of them have the moral courage to admit it, that the refusal to Germany of colonies, if persisted in, will inevitably lead to another war. Who in his senses can believe that a Great Power, with so enormous a commercial stake in the world and so virile and intelligent a population, which increases while that of France decreases, will, after its forty years' experience of overseas empire, be content to acquiesce permanently in the present distribution of the undeveloped native territories of Africa? It cannot be inopportune to recall some striking facts and figures bearing on this subject. Before the war Germany amongst the seven Colonial States of Europe[9] had the largest home population, the fourth highest density of home population, the fourth highest rate of natural increase of population, the largest number of home inhabitants to every square mile of colonial territory, and, conversely, the smallest ratio of oversea empire to home population. Further, while since 1871 the density of population had increased in France from 171 to only 190 inhabitants to the square mile, the corresponding increase in Germany had been from 110 to 310. The peace arrangements have made more glaring the privileged position of the other colonial Powers, four of which have benefited by the war - in three cases directly, and in the fourth indirectly, at Germany's expense.

It is inconceivable, however, that Belgium, with a population of seven and a quarter millions, should have an empire of nearly a million square miles; that a decadent country like Portugal, with a population of six millions, should have an empire of equal extent; that France, with a population of 38 millions at the most,[10] which is far from large enough for her home needs, should have an empire of nearly five million square miles; while Germany, the third greatest industrial country in the world, with still a prolific population of some sixty-five millions, should be doomed to perpetual exclusion from the ranks of colonial Powers. Those who hold that such an inequitable status can last are welcome to their belief, but it is perilous to stake the peace of the world upon a hypothesis so slight. As late as April 10, 1916, Mr. Asquith publicly declared: "The aim of the Allies in this war is to smooth the path towards an international system ensuring the principle of *equal rights for all civilized nations.*" The colonial stipulations of the Treaty of Versailles are a mockery of that just principle.

It is not merely a British interest in the truest sense, but a European and a world interest, that this untenable incongruity should not continue. Count Beust, as Austrian Foreign Minister, once formulated what may be called the law of territorial constriction when, alluding to the attempt to bind Russia against her will and interest by the letter of an obsolete treaty, he wrote: *"Toute compression excessive a pour effet de provoquer l'expansion dans une autre direction"* (Dispatch of January 1, 1867). It was the recognition of this fact that led Bismarck, after the war of 1870, to encourage France to indulge her colonial ambitions in any direction she pleased, for he argued astutely that the more she looked outward from Europe the less would be her pressure upon Germany, particularly in the matter of Alsace-Lorraine. The Wise Men of Gotham who concocted the Treaty of Versailles pretended to know better, and closed all Germany's outlets, fatuously believing that their little bolts and padlocks would withstand the hand of Time.

Those who suppose that Germany will settle down to the loss of her colonies are deceiving themselves and others. Should we in like circumstances? To ask that question is to answer it. But why should we expect the Germans to act differently than ourselves? And why should the colonial stipulations of the Treaty of Versailles be more binding upon Germany than the territorial provisions of the Treaty of Frankfort were held, with our approval, to be in the case of France? Surely not because the former was forced upon a beaten adversary without parley, while the latter was laboriously negotiated, article by article, through weeks and months? Count Brockdoff-Rantzau, who, though the head of the German Delegation, refused to sign the Treaty of Versailles, said of the Allied Governments in the Weimar National Assembly: "They can apply force to us, but they cannot compel us to recognize force as law." In these words, by which the entire German nation stands, and rightly stands, he did but restate a maxim of jurisprudence which is approved by the conscience of the civilized world.

It is not enough that the retention of Germany's colonies will inevitably bring about another war, but by their action in this matter the Allied nations have given to the evil principles of conquest and revenge a sanction more formal, deliberate, and definite than ever before, and one which would justify future victors in war in proceeding to any extremes of annexation and oppression. Incidentally, it is worth while to remember that the re-seizure by France of the Congo territory ceded to Germany in 1911 in consideration of her recognition of the priority of French influence in Morocco - a recognition given by Great Britain in return for freedom of action in Egypt - has upset the North African settlement, so opening up possibilities of renewed trouble in that part of the world whenever Germany shall be able and disposed to reassert the rights of a Great Power.

The country which most suspiciously and most naturally holds back from disarmament proposals does so for the best of all reasons - that the Peace of Versailles is not a peace of reconciliation and security but one of unexampled aggravation and the sure prelude of future armed strife. The tragedy is that the Allied Governments and nations have so far refused to face the only alternatives to a prospect so terrible yet so real. For Pascal was not altogether cynical when he wrote in his *Pensées* that "*l'homme ne veut pas qu'on lui dit la verité, il évite de la dire aux autres.*" It is true that all sorts of peddling little devices for promoting international amity are discussed whenever the League of Nations Assembly meets - congresses of parliamentary delegations, exchanges of teachers and scholars, revisions of history teaching, the moralizing of the Press, and the rest. All these things are laudable, and in the measure of their influence they may be helpful to the end desired, but none of them will touch the deeper springs of national feeling, least of all in those countries which have seen their territories hacked and hewn with the cold brutality of a headsman's axe. Even the Pact of Locarno, so greatly to be welcomed as an earnest of returning European sanity, is only a symbol of the greater Treaty of Revision which will be necessary if the nations of the Continent are to settle down and we ourselves are to hope for any permanent revival of the old prosperity. For cautious politicians, only too painfully conscious of the limited value of the diplomatic *petits soins* of euphemistic language and elegant courtesies, it is thus less the substance of the Locarno negotiations and Pact than the spirit behind, and the will to make this first real adventure in reconciliation, that are of consequence. None the less, there has come to Sir Austen Chamberlain the opportunity of performing that still greater and more abiding work for European peace which the authors of the Versailles Treaty threw away. Let him, continuing on the good way he has entered, follow his excellent principles by practical measures, and the gratitude of his contemporaries and the blessings of posterity, forfeited by them, may fall to him. The after-war *rôle* of a Lincoln is still unfilled in Europe.

To no country in the world is the question of tranquillity and security so vital as to Great Britain, whose great need and interest is not the extension of her empire, but its consolidation and development, a task hardly as yet seriously faced and more than sufficient to tax all her available administrative capacity, commercial enterprise, and material resource, without adding to her responsibilities vast areas of two continents. Whatever may be the case with the islands of the Pacific and the portion of South-West Africa bordering on British territories, we had no need of either German East Africa, the seizure of which has already brought upon us a Nemesis in the form of a grave Indian problem, nor yet of Togo and the part of the Cameroons, in the west of the continent, which we likewise bespoke as spoil so early as 1916. Perhaps no greater disservice was ever done to the British Empire than this arbitrary extension of its bounds and liabilities in a spirit of sheer cupidity, for it concentrated the world's attention upon the Empire - by no means sympathetically, whatever may be the language of diplomacy - as a never-sated dominion, and invited comparisons with less fortunate countries which could not by any possibility be to our advantage. It is not I who say this - it is what is said all over the world, and by our late Allies quite as much as by neutral nations, as anyone who follows foreign opinion may see for himself.

As if to give new force to what is here said, while this Introduction was in the press the newspapers published from Lisbon the following telegram, dated December 23rd (I quote from *The Times*):

> "The (Portuguese) Minister for Foreign Affairs has read to the Chamber of Deputies a telegram received from the Portuguese Ambassador in London in which he reproduced a Note received from the British Foreign Office, giving a formal assurance that there was no truth in the recent allegations in the Portuguese and foreign Press that Great Britain has designs, or encourages the designs of others, against the Portuguese colonies."

How many readers of that statement felt the sting of the reproach implied by the inquiry whether our Government contemplated robbery or was inciting other Governments thereto? While not overweighting the significance of the report which the Foreign Secretary has had to contradict - an act on his part which must be unique in the history of his great Department - the important fact to be taken to heart is that suspicions so unworthy of this country should have been entertained at all by minds naturally friendly to us. What was held to justify these suspicions? The Anglo-German treaty of 1898, providing for the partition of Portugal's colonies between the two Powers in the event of their coming into the market, created a bad impression, and this the unratified revised treaty of 1914 cannot have removed; but at least these agreements, if in dubious taste, were not aggressive. Is there not evidence here of a lessened confidence in British faith, and for this is it not clear that we must go to the proceedings at Versailles in 1919? With all earnestness I would say that, in the changed temper of our restless modern world, it is not good or safe for the Empire that the faintest ground should exist for distrust of this kind.

It is also a deplorable fact that even at home the cause of Imperialism, even of the sober kind, no longer holds the imagination and sympathy of the masses of the people in the degree it did before a war which began with the renunciation of all idea of territorial greed and ended with a surfeit of that ugly passion. Those who condemn the Trade Union Congress for having recently passed with practical unanimity (for the card vote showed 3,820,000 votes against 79,000) so strong a resolution against colonization in general as at present practised might charitably ask themselves what was bound to be the effect of the bartering of native populations under the Treaty of Versailles, not to speak of the later Jubaland Pact, upon the minds of the millions of the toiling class - men and women who on the whole, whatever the immaturity of their judgments on large social and economic issues, do unquestionably in their political thinking come nearer to the basic principles of human justice, and on purely moral questions are more instinctively right, than their so-called betters. For do they misrepresent facts when they tell us that European Imperialism to-day rests more than ever on arbitrary force? A strong "civilized" nation invades independent native territory, proclaims a protectorate against the protest of its inhabitants, then when these unwilling "subjects" rudely resort to active protest declares them to be "rebels" and summarily suppresses them by machine guns, aeroplane bombs, and poison gas.[11] Is not that the sequence of events in Morocco and Syria at the present time? And whence come the voices raised in protest? Who hears them?

For myself, who was never other than an Imperialist, albeit of the Eighth-Commandment type, while believing as strongly as ever in the British Empire as a great and potent instrument of civilization, and, in spite of all past and present shortcomings, as an unexampled blessing to the human race, I hold that its fair fame has been injured by these shabby annexations. It is not the fault of the Empire, of course, but of the men who were untrue to its best traditions.

"Great Britain has a full share of responsibilities in the African continent," wrote before the war one of the acutest and most level-headed of British statesmen. Then why in the name of reason was this heavy and wholly unnecessary addition made to the load? The most willing of workers can only exert himself wisely, or for others beneficially, within the measure of his strength. Cannot the national ambition, enterprise and spirit of adventure of the British peoples be satisfied by giving more attention to the colonizing tasks which have fallen to us as so clearly our very own, and doing that work better than in the past, leaving something for other nations not so heavily encumbered to do? One of Dr. Schnee's greatest countrymen, whom this country has reason to remember with respect, Wilhelm von Humboldt, wrote over a hundred years ago that "in government England remains an unattainable model," and we are perhaps still justified in accepting the compliment, always with due modesty. But that is no reason why we should grudge to other peoples a fair share in the work of civilization, which is the rightful business and duty of all nations which are themselves civilized. "Not this man and that man, but all men, make up mankind, and their united tasks the tasks of mankind." Carlyle's words apply no less to nations, their relationships and duties to each other and the entire human race.

There is also the money aspect of the question. Germany expended millions of pounds on the development of her colonies, and was still spending huge sums on railways, harbour works, and the like. Why should the British taxpayers, who already finance the Dominions, the Indian Dependency, and the Crown Colonies to so large an extent, be required to undertake new liabilities of this kind, and who will maintain that the return would ever justify the expenditure?

That the German colonies have so far benefited by the change of rule is a very disputable question; the evidence assembled in the following pages makes it clear that in some territories there have been confusion and retrogression in many directions. In some matters the results have been altogether and irreparably bad. Sanitation, for example, has fallen back disastrously. Further, large territories which formerly, under German rule, were open to the free commerce of the world, without preference or privilege, are now, in French hands, more or less closed preserves, to which merchandise other than French is admitted only, if at all, subject to excessive duties.

It is in the territories which have passed under French rule that the most deplorable evil of all has been introduced. Under her mandates, in direct violation both of the spirit and the letter of the Covenant of the League of Nations, and of the conditions applying to all other mandated territories, France has been given the monstrous liberty to militarize the native populations committed to her care as "a sacred trust of civilization," and actually to employ the black armies so raised in future European battlefields. France has lost no time in submitting her new black subjects to military training, enrolling them in her armies, and even employing them in the little wars which are being waged in other parts of her empire.

Do the people of these islands endorse this policy? In a speech made in the House of Commons on August 8, 1918, Mr. (now Lord) Balfour, speaking as Foreign Secretary, said:

> *"I raise no abstract objection to the creation of a black army - that is right or wrong according to circumstances.* What I object to is giving back to Germany at the end of the war an instrument so powerful for evil as a great colonial army would be in German hands."

Without considering the question whether in the words italicized Lord Balfour reflected the moral sense of any large body of Englishmen, I would ask fair-minded readers to remember that the innuendo contained in the latter part of the quotation was not justified by anything that had happened in the past, for Germany never militarized her native territories; only France has done that. Further, some months before Mr. Balfour spoke, Dr. Solf, whose reputation as a colonial governor was of the highest,[12] and who was then Colonial Secretary, explicitly disavowed any such policy in future. He said on December 21, 1917:

> "I am the only German Minister in office who has spoken about the militarization of Africa - in Leipzig, recently - *and what I said was exactly the opposite, namely, that we do **not** desire the militarization of the black races of Africa.* The best way of preventing such militarization of the black races is to agree to the new partitioning of the Continent which we ask for. If an equipoise of power all round is substituted for the unequal distribution which has prevailed hitherto, it ceases to be possible for any one colonial Power to transport black forces to Europe without exposing the colony to the danger of an attack by the equally strong neighbour Power. But the interest which any Power may have in organizing native armies will be very much diminished when there can no longer be any question of employing them in

Europe or anywhere outside the colonies. *Since, however, our attitude to the whole question is one of principle, we shall be ready to go farther and promote any limitation by agreement in Africa.*"[13]

Nevertheless, in spite of these clear and authoritative words, which had been published in English newspapers and quoted in the Introduction to Mr. Edwyn Bevan's book already named, Lord Balfour, while silent as to the actual policy of France, which had already militarized her native territories and had sent black armies to Europe, attributed to Germany a design which had been officially disclaimed, and did this for the purpose of justifying the annexation of her colonies.

More than ever before the "instrument so powerful for evil" has been put in the hands of France by the Allied Governments, our own amongst them, and France is using it for evil. The employment of blacks - in the case of France by coercive methods, as Dr. Schnee, quoting from French sources, shows - to do the fighting of white nations is an abominable perversion of any true conception of "a sacred trust of civilization." Here are some figures which give rise to reflexion. In a statement made on December 23, 1925, before the Financial Affairs Committee of the Chamber of Deputies, on the credits for Morocco and Syria, M. Painlevé said that "the fatalities in the Moroccan campaign, from the beginning to date, had been 2,640, of whom only 920, or 35 per cent., were Frenchmen; while of 8,779 wounded and missing 2,304, or only 26 per cent., were Frenchmen. The casualties amongst other than Frenchmen would, of course, comprise members of the Foreign Legion besides the more numerous native soldiers, but no separate figures were given.

Quite recently France employed her dusky North African, Senegalese, and other natives in the dragooning of Western Germany, by that act outraging the moral sense of the whole world - friends in America have assured me that nothing has more estranged American sympathy from France than this act - and should France and Germany again come to blows the Germans might find themselves in actual warfare with their former subjects, whom they have done so much to civilize. But might not worse happen in the future? Who, with a knowledge of the attitude of France towards our own country during the thirty years preceding the conclusion of the Dual Entente, and remembering how fragile French friendship is apt to prove when weighed in the scales against material interest, will dare to say that these black armies might not one day be used against her present Allies? While no pessimist, and while fully recognizing the importance of amicable relations with France - a true union of hearts there will never be - it is my profound conviction that in identifying our national policy and interests so closely and emphatically with those of France we are once again "backing the wrong horse." This distrust springs not merely from a dislike of alliances of every kind and degree, but still more from an old-fashioned habit of paying heed to the warnings of history, and hence from recognition of the fact that whereas from the founding of the German Empire in 1871 down to 1904 the successive Governments of that country never seriously stood in Great Britain's way on territorial questions, but consistently met us in a conciliatory and accommodating spirit, sometimes easing our difficulties enormously, as on the Egyptian question, France for the greater part of that time just as systematically did the reverse. The inner history of that period, when it comes to be written by the aid of unpublished dispatches, both those in public and those in private hands, will be a revelation to the next generation. Existing biographies and memorials of contemporary diplomats and statesmen already give an earnest of what may be expected. Lord Newton's *Life of Lord Lyons* (1913) may be cited in illustration.

Is it certain that the future will bring no repetition of the past? Those optimists who think that national characteristics can be changed in a year, a decade, or even a generation, have yet to begin the study of folk-psychology. Guizot wrote at the end of 1852, just after the Prince-President had been declared Emperor as Napoleon III: "Our country is a prey to two contradictory cravings, a craving for repose and a craving for new and violent emotions. She wishes to have her interests secured, but also to have her imagination satisfied at the same time." The words faithfully indicate a temperament and a constant conflict of impulses which in the case of France European statesmen never dare to lose sight of. The craving for military glory may often slumber in French breasts, but sooner or later it breaks out afresh; and always glory of that sort is gained by one nation at the cost and to the hurt of another nation. And it is true, as the historian of modern France writes, that "the issues which divide or unite nations are regulated by unexpected contingencies which defy even the calculations of statesmen and divert the patriotic passions of peoples."

To pursue that question now, however, would be premature and futile. The British nation prefers always to learn its lessons in foreign policy in the school of chastening experience, and of a surety it will learn this lesson in due time. All I would say further on this subject is that no greater blunder could be committed by this country than to permanently alienate the German nation. The Allies have professed to put Germany in Coventry: let us take heed lest the time should come when Germany, forced to seek new friends and finding them, either in Europe or Asia, should be able to turn the tables upon her present oppressors, saying, like Coriolanus to the smug Roman citizens, "I banish you!" For the idea that such a nation can for ever, or for long, be held down is childish. In Swift's well-known story the pigmies of Lilliput regarded Gulliver, pegged down to the ground with their little pins and cords, as their prisoner at will, never dreaming that with a single turn the giant would be free. Similarly, small minds persist in regarding Germany as held in duress from which she cannot hope to escape. It is a foolish and fatal delusion, from which there will one day be a rude awakening.

I am no alarmist, but I make the confession, for what it is worth, that in my view Germany after the Treaty of Versailles is far more to be feared, both politically and economically, than ever she was before. Every statesman worthy of the name suspects it, but because the danger is not immediate, and may not be acute for a decade or two, it is counted wise policy to conceal the truth from the people; for in England to dispel a popular illusion is a greater crime than to break one of the Commandments. I see the Germany of fifty years hence - and fifty years are but as a day in a nation's history - a powerful and opulent State, perhaps long before then an Empire again, though still under democratic rule, with a population of a hundred millions, the most vigorous of the Continent.[14] And France - will she have fifty or only thirty millions, as may well happen if the dry-rot in her social system be not stayed? As for the British Empire, can we be quite sure, however ardently we may hope it, that it will still be an undivided unity? In any event, does anyone believe that Canada and Australia would fight for the retention of unneeded and disputed territory in East and West Africa? Anticipating such possibilities, are not the risks involved in the grasping policy pursued in 1919 too great? If we are incapable of generosity, let us at least be intelligent, and make from considerations of prudence and interest a renunciation which we may refuse to make from higher motives.

Already, indeed, we have a foretaste of what the policy of unreasoning repression is doing for that country and for us. We see it in Germany's frantic efforts to rehabilitate her industrial system and prestige, in her unequalled concentration upon and devotion to work, in the anxiety and trepidation occasioned by her every movement on the political chessboard of Europe. In 1917, while the war was at its height and it was still an open question whether conciliation or rancour, wisdom or folly, would eventually determine the peace settlement, I wrote, criticizing the wild and vindictive penal measures - so much more numerous than those of moderation and sanity - which were already proposed for Germany's benefit:

> "The more the proposals of retaliation and revenge are considered, the more will they be seen to offer no hope whatever of achieving the purpose which their authors have in view - the crippling of Germany either as a commercial or a political Power.... The surest way of stimulating Germany to the exercise of her greatest energies is to try to keep her under humiliating restraints.

That is the way of human nature, and it will not alter for our convenience. Cobden wrote many words of wisdom when the Allies were endeavouring to reduce Russia in the Crimean War, and these were among them: 'In estimating the difficulties of our task when undertaking to subdue such an empire to our will, it is necessary not only to ascertain the extent of suffering and privation we can inflict on its population, but *the amount of mental force we evoke to sustain them in its endurance.*' In spite of warnings from all sorts of sources, the British nation insisted on taking Germany too cheaply before the war and there is a danger that the mistake may be repeated after it.... Half the mistakes by the Allies in the conduct of the war, and particularly their miscalculations and want of foresight, have been due to a disposition to underrate Germany's strength in man-power, material-power, and above all, will-power. Clever theorists have persisted in confusing men with statistics and statistics with men, forgetting that it is the spirit of a nation that count first, last, and all the time. How obvious this truth is, yet how persistently it is ignored!... For myself, I should fear Germany more as a bound than a free country, and that is why I see in the policy of repression and restraint only an infinite potentiality of mischief and danger."[15]

Were these warnings necessary, or not? Hatred, rancour, violence, cupidity triumphed at Versailles, and we are to-day paying the penalty, and we shall continue to pay it until wisdom recovers unchallenged sway in the counsels of the nations, for then only shall we truly seek peace and ensue it. The bitter fact is that, beaten and for the moment held in restraint though she is, Germany today dominates the European stage, and conditions the peace of the Continent, in a way she never did under the Empire. The deprivations of territory imposed upon her were to have weakened her beyond hope of recovery: what they have done is to steel her spirit and inflame her nationalist fires. The hundred and one economic handicaps - some senselessly cruel, others still more senselessly petty and childish - which were to have disabled her as an industrial rival are having the effect of stimulating her exertions, enterprise, ingenuity, inventiveness, and resource in every direction, with results which are forcing themselves upon the least reflective mind. In 1914 the world was beginning to weary of super-men and super-nations; but the statesmen who devised the fearful and wonderful Treaty of Versailles have done their best to create conditions which promise to evolve a State that will not only become an economic colossus amongst its fellows, but will have the power - and might in conceivable circumstances use it - to keep the whole of Europe for an indefinite time on the tenterhooks of apprehension and alarm, and to throw back for generations the inspiring ideal of a New World and a humaner civilization, the achievement of which was to have crowned and consecrated the most terrible war of history.

The truth is that the clever men who forced upon Germany the Treaty of Versailles, and therewith sacrificed the moral gains of the war, wanted to make history and to make it quickly. They made it, and it has proved very bad history, so much so that a good part of it will have to be remade. And what have the victorious nations gained in return for the follies done in their name? To recall again some wise words of Cobden: "It would be very monstrous indeed in the moral government of the world if one class of the community could permanently benefit at the expense of the misery and suffering of the rest." It is just the same with nations: every one of us knows and sees and feels it to-day. For while the money penalty imposed on Germany has had to be reduced, as demonstrably excessive, the penalty her victors are paying, heavy as it is, tends to increase. What is their plight, seven dismal years after the end of the war? Take only the Great Powers of the Entente. Russia is a heap of ruins. Of the other Allies, three are in dire financial straits, their nationals in the mass impoverished owing to the depreciation of their currency to the extent of 75 and 80 per cent, and their working classes required to work longer hours for less pay; while our own country is struggling under the threefold burden of excessive taxation, high prices, and an unparalleled volume of unemployment, most of which threatens to be permanent. "Simply the natural play of economic forces," comments the materialistic philosopher, to whom the world is an ingenious piece of machinery with a disagreeable habit of getting out of order. Granting that most of the present social ills of Europe can be traced to visible economic causes and reactions, is it not clear that even on the low material plane policies of rancour and revenge do not pay in international dealings? What is the hope - or is there none? Those who believe that the universe is something more than a gaming board and human beings more than counters must also believe that it can never be right with men or nations unless they do right. In the long run selfishness and cupidity cannot prosper, for they are self-sterile, self-destructive.

I come to the conclusion of the matter. That the Treaty of Versailles - and not that Peace Treaty alone - will be radically revised sooner or later no one with even a glimmering of political insight and prescience has ever doubted. It is for statesmen to decide how the revision shall come about - whether by the rude way of nature, which so often effaces the effects of one cataclysm by a still greater cataclysm, or by the transforming influence of a new spirit of morality, conciliation, and amity amongst the nations. One of the directions in which revision is most urgent is the restoration of colonies to Germany. Why not begin here, the more since it is essentially a matter of the reapportionment of the Mandates, coupled with such supplementary territorial readjustments as the Allied Powers might arrange amongst themselves? There is reason to believe that any agreement acceptable to the Allied Powers on the Mandate question would have the general endorsement of the other States represented in the League of Nations, not a few of which would bless the act and hour that removed so potent a source of present discord and future disturbance from the political arena.

But why does Germany need colonies? Why do we need them - why does France or Belgium? Quite as much as any of the colonial Powers of Europe, and far more than most of them, Germany, as a nation of expanding population and industry, needs outlets for the former and for the latter, besides markets, an independent supply of such raw materials as tropical countries alone supply, under her direct control. The population question may not be specially urgent at the moment, but that cannot be said of the other. It would be easy to cite many impartial testimonies on both of these subjects, but I take one only because of the reputation of the author. In a book published on the eve of the war Sir Harry Johnston stated the issue fairly when, after showing how Germany was losing to other nations her surplus population, he wrote:

> "'*You* may well be content,' is the German cry addressed to Great Britain, 'for *you* have occupied or earmarked such an enormous proportion of the earth's surface that you do not need to talk of extension for three centuries to come. *We* may have provided sufficient elbow room for the next twenty years, but that is not sufficient. Instinctively we must fight for the future, or our memories will be reproached by our children and our children's children.' This may be called 'sentimental nonsense,' because it is uttered by Germans and not by Englishmen. But we are the last of the Powers who should laugh at such a yearning. Moreover, the Germans, after all, are only expressing a divine afflatus, the determination of the best type of man to dominate the world.
>
> "The German people as a whole are resolved upon colonial expansion for two reasons. The first is that their country is far from producing naturally the bulk of the raw products required for their industries, and they desire to assure to themselves for the future a special control over, or access to, undeveloped regions in Asia, Africa, and America, where these raw products can be obtained or where they can be cultivated; secondly, they require to be certain, in these days of the growth of empires, that a sufficient portion of the earth's habitable area will remain free and open for the sale of German manufactured goods or industrial products."[16]

I do not forget that later, influenced by the invasion of Belgium, Sir Harry Johnston seemed to recant the view expressed above, though while respecting his courage I failed at the time to follow his logic. Nevertheless, whatever views we may hold regarding that illegal act or, in the light of fuller knowledge, the larger question of responsibility for the war,[17] the position of Germany to-day is still as this authority on colonization described it twelve years ago, and to refuse to recognize this fact is to seek certain trouble. The question of outlets for surplus population is beset by special difficulties, but it is not involved in the problem discussed in these pages, since none of the territories taken from Germany during the war offers any large scope for a white population. As a German colonial authority has said of these territories, the fertile ones are in general unhealthy, while the healthy ones are unfertile. My own opinion is that this larger problem might be best solved by an agreement with Brazil for the establishment at some future time of a politically independent German democratic State as part of that vast and sparsely populated territory. Such an arrangement, since it would not raise the Monroe Doctrine as hitherto understood, should not provoke hostility in the United States, particularly if the American Government were consulted beforehand and were kept informed of all subsequent negotiations. The German claim to the restoration of colonies on economic grounds is more urgent, and cannot be faced too soon.

There is no reason why the colonial tangle which we have unwisely created for ourselves should not be unravelled by the process of sensible bargaining, in which not only Great Britain, France, and Germany, but Belgium, Portugal, and Italy, as equally custodians of vast African territories, might all take part. Germany tells us that she needs a consolidated colonial empire, and that is our own position in South Africa and the Pacific. The acceptance of that principle should afford the basis of an arrangement satisfactory to every rightful claim. Germany's needs could well be met in tropical Africa, the mandated territories in the east and west of the continent being returned as a minimum. On what conditions - whether by exchange of territory or an abatement of the indemnity -South-West Africa and the Pacific Islands, which were wrested from Germany, should be retained for the British Empire, as is desirable, is a question which would form part of such an all-round settlement; since it is a vital necessity that the tenure of these lands, now resting only on the unstable foundations of conquest and a forced treaty, devoid of legal or moral sanction, should be amicably regularized. If it should be said that it would now be difficult to return, say, Tanganyika to Germany because many British subjects have since bought estates and settled there, the answer is that in appropriating this territory we did an inexcusably foolhardy thing in the face of ample warning, and further that our Government was not in the least squeamish when, for political reasons, it was found expedient to hand over Jubaland to Italy and other African territory to Belgium, though the transfer of British nationals to new sovereignty was similarly involved in each case. Disinterested neutral nations might be disposed to remind us that no disturbances of the kind which the reinstatement of Germany in her colonies would entail could compare with the sufferings inflicted upon the thousands of innocent Germans who, after first being despoiled of their properties, were summarily exiled from the countries which they had done so much to develop and civilize.

But what about British interests and security? In our rightful concern for these let us not be blind to the fact that there are other interests in the world besides our own, and that these have an equal right to consideration. "Tell me now," said Gortchakoff to the British ambassador in St. Petersburg in a critical moment during the Anglo-Russian tension in 1877, "tell me now, what are those British interests which are threatened?" The ambassador answered in the good old diplomatic way that "England must be the judge of her own interests." That sort of quibbling is no longer possible to-day. Legitimate interests are not established by any Power vis-à-vis its neighbours, still less the world at large, by simply asserting that they exist. But does the security of the Empire require that Germany shall have no colonies? Is it not obvious that its tranquillity and security would be imperilled in the highest degree by reverting to the dog-in-the-manger policy towards Germany which we followed for a time on this question in 1884-5, to the permanent injury of good relations between the two countries? Who that has taken the trouble to acquaint himself with the depth and strength of the colonial sentiment in Germany can doubt that if the policy of keeping Germany out of Africa is to be maintained, the peace of Europe will be under constant menace? In 1905 and 1911 we risked war with Germany in order to secure Morocco for France, which has no surplus population wherewith to colonize, and does not, in fact, colonize at all? Even an admirer of France so wholehearted as Mr. Bodley permits himself to speak of her colonies as "so-called." Is it wise, politic, statesmanlike to make certain a future war with Germany, in which we might stand alone, by persisting in retaining the territories which the Germans have done so much to develop and the possession of which they regard as essential alike to their economic prosperity and their national honour?

Is it not, rather, true, as Mr. Bonar Law said in the House of Commons on one occasion, that "the British Empire is large enough already, and our true interest is to develop what we have"? It is even more to the interest of the Empire now than in the past that Germany should have all reasonable scope for colonial expansion, since by endeavouring to limit her needlessly we should increase the difficulties of our own position abroad. To withhold colonies from Germany would be a declaration of war against her national aspirations. Are we prepared to face the consequences of such an attitude, and is any gain that it may promise worth the risk? On the other hand, a policy of conciliation upon this question would justify itself abundantly. There is no reason in the world why, in addition to the hostility and resentment of our late antagonists which we share in common with our Allies over the general issues of the war, we should go out of our way to earn an extra portion on our own account over the colonial question. Whether they like it or not, Great Britain and Germany will again be neighbours in the future, and our action in this, perhaps more than in any other matter, will decide whether they shall be tolerably good neighbours or intolerably bad ones. To meet Germany in a conciliatory spirit on this question, and to do it voluntarily, so anticipating the risk of external pressure, would do very much to placate her national pride and to assuage the bitterness inseparable from defeat in war. We might thereby hope to succeed in dislodging from German and other minds - and it would be well worth our while - that disposition to regard the British Empire as a proper object of envy and covetousness which has been so prevalent in the past and has been further encouraged by the ill-considered action taken in 1919.

If France and Belgium wish to take the risk, let them do it alone and stand the consequences; there is no reason why British flesh and blood should be hazarded in a cause which is not worth fighting for. The likelihood is, however, that if Great Britain agreed to renounce her East and West African mandates in Germany's favour, France would promptly follow her example, glad to be gracefully released from an impossible position. It is gratifying to know that already many sober voices have been raised in France urging that this country should take the lead in the matter. I quote only one, that of M. Jean Finot, who wrote in the *Revue Mondiale* a short time ago:

> "There is only one way of promoting the early recovery of Germany, and that is by restoring her colonies. If England would agree to that, she would give to the world an example of great self-conquest and truly humane purposes. The German nation would then be able to develop peaceably, and could satisfy in oversea territories its superfluous force and its longing for expansion. The English friends of Germany make a somewhat pitiable spectacle when they confine their sympathy to mere words and show no disposition to perform an act which would be one both of clemency and of the highest justice."

In the mass we British, to whatever part of the island realm we may belong, are a very self-centred people, who in foreign affairs seldom take the trouble to view questions from any other standpoint but our own, and even so resolutely refuse to take long views. Elsewhere I have called attention to a monumental illustration of the narrow outlook of our statesmanship in relation to the appearance in the European arena in the middle of last century of the very State with which this book is concerned.[18] At that time and for years later hardly one of the statesmen responsible for the determination of British foreign policy troubled about Germany or knew anything about her: few statesmen of the present day know much, even after the war. Just as then, so since, we have persisted in closing our eyes to all foreign problems save those of the immediate present, taking no thought for the morrow, facing difficulties only when they could no longer be evaded, occasionally incurring liabilities light-heartedly without suspecting their meaning. So it came about that July, 1914, found us committed to the greatest national crisis of our history, yet nevertheless wondering how it could possibly have happened.

Has the same old policy of blindness, apathy, and inertia to be followed in regard to this colonial problem, which short-sighted men have needlessly created, and which cannot by any possibility be solved by merely ignoring it and waiting on events? Shall we once more trust to our luck when complications arise, as sooner or later they will arise unless we act promptly and judiciously, and hope that, somehow or other, we shall successfully "bungle through"? With no other interests to serve save justice, sound policy, and the safety and welfare of our common country and of the Empire, I for one utter again the urgent warning which wisdom justifies and patriotism demands. A private individual, standing outside party politics and controversies, can do no more.

W. H. DAWSON.

Headington, Oxford,
    December 1925.

Scenery at Dar-es-Salam, German East Africa.

Scenery at Windhoek, South-West Africa.

2

Biographical Note: Dr. Schnee

Dr. Heinrich Schnee was born in 1871 at Neuhaldensleben, near Magdeburg, and after passing through the Nordhausen Gymnasium studied at the universities of Heidelberg, Kiel, and Berlin, as well as the Oriental Seminary in Berlin, where he specialized in colonial administration and the Suaheli language, his intention being to follow a colonial career. In 1892 he passed his Referendary examination; in the following year he took his degree of Doctor of Laws; in 1897 he passed his examination as Government Assessor and joined the Colonial Department of the Foreign Office; in 1898 he was appointed Resident Magistrate and Deputy Governor in German New Guinea; and two years later he became District Administrator and Deputy-Governor in Samoa.

While functioning in New Guinea, whose native inhabitants still lived in a condition of anarchy and cannibalism, it was his endeavour, by the appointment of native chiefs, to create orderly conditions and to suppress the barbarous customs and habits of the aborigines. He gave much attention to research into native customs and languages in the South Seas, publishing essays thereon in scientific journals, and he visited British, Dutch, and American colonies.

In 1904 Dr. Schnee became Councillor of Legation in the Foreign Office (Colonial Department); in 1905 he was attached to the German Embassy in London as Colonial Councillor; in 1906 he became "Real"

Councillor of Legation in the Colonial Department; in 1907, Director of the same; in 1911, Ministerial Director and head of the Political and Administrative Division of the Imperial Colonial Office (created in 1907); and from 1912 to 1919 he was Governor of German East Africa.

As a Colonial Administrator Dr. Schnee at all times made it his aim to promote the elevation of the native population. He attached great importance to the cultivation of the closest personal contact with the natives, to which end he frequently travelled through the territories under his care, and acquired four native languages (Malay, the language of the inhabitants of the Gazelle Peninsula of New Pomerania, Samoan, and Suaheli). In German East Africa he introduced legislation for the protection of the native labourers against exploitation and ill-treatment, and he also initiated far-going sanitary regulations on their behalf. Further, he did much for the stamping out of disease in man and beast; in particular he applied systematically Robert Koch's method of combating Sleeping Sickness, and established at Mpapua the Veterinary Institute for combating Rinderpest and other diseases to which domestic animals were subject. He likewise did much for the extension and improvement of native instruction, establishing schools for artisans, experimental stations from which seeds and plants were supplied free to the natives, and other institutions for the benefit of the latter.

In German East Africa he followed Baron von Rechenberg, who is likewise known as a man who brought a humane spirit and outlook to the performance of his duties as Governor, and who had nearly completed six years of activity from which the interests of the natives greatly benefited. Dr. Schnee carried on the administration in the same spirit, and with a success evidenced by the fact that from 1906 to 1914 no rising occurred, nor did any occur during the war, an immunity which was not enjoyed by the adjacent colonies.

In recognition of his merits in the sphere of colonial affairs, scientific and otherwise, Dr. Schnee in 1919 was awarded by the Prussian Academy of Sciences the Leibniz medal in gold, and two years later the University of Hamburg conferred upon him the degree of Doctor of

DR. HEINRICH SCHNEE

Political Sciences, special mention being made in the diploma of the humane spirit in which he had filled the office of Colonial Governor.

Dr. Schnee has made important contributions to the literature of colonization, including *Pictures from the South Sea* (1904), *Our Colonies* (1908), and *German East Africa in the World War* (1919), and he also edited the *German Colonial Lexikon*, in three volumes (1920). Since 1924 he has been a member of the Reichstag, belonging to the German People's Party, and in 1925 he was elected Senator of the German Academy in Munich. His wife is an English lady, formerly resident in New Zealand. Their home is at 11 Lietzenseeufer, Berlin-Charlottenburg.

3

How the German Colonies Were Seized

By the Treaty of Versailles, which was not negotiated, as treaties of peace traditionally are, but drawn up by the representatives of the Allied Powers and forced on a disarmed enemy, Germany was required to surrender her colonies. The Powers whose troops occupied those colonies in the course of the war had already divided them amongst themselves. In accordance with the provisions of the treaty named they have since governed the whole of Germany's oversea territories under mandate of the League of Nations, in whose name they are supposed to act.

Laborious attempts have been made to justify the appropriation of the German colonies before the world by the plea that Germany had shown herself unfit to colonize and unworthy of possessing colonies. Grave accusations have been levelled against German colonial activity. In particular, Germany has been accused of militarizing her colonies in such a way as to become a menace to other nations, and of ill-treating the native populations. An elaborately planned indictment of Germany's "colonial guilt" has, in fact, been built up, in the hope of establishing the claim that it would be "impossible" to entrust my country and nation again with responsibility for the fate of the colonies and of their native populations.

It is the purpose of these chapters to meet this indictment, to disclose the methods adopted in framing it, and to prove its baselessness. For there rests upon the German nation just the same necessity of refuting the ungenerous fiction of "colonial guilt" as of repudiating the charge that it alone must bear responsibility for the late war - a charge now made with ever-diminishing assurance even by those who still adhere to it, and abandoned altogether by most well-informed students of pre-war documentary and circumstantial evidence, both in neutral and combatant countries.

We Germans owe it to ourselves and to our children, we owe it to our position amongst the nations, that these reflections upon our national honour should be rebutted before all the world. We also owe it to the future of our race, in order that the way may be cleared for the return of Germany to the ranks of colonizing nations, since without colonies our country can never develop to the full its economic resources or play its rightful part, and the part for which it has abundantly proved its capacity, in the industrial and commercial life of the world.

Not less, however, do our late enemies, if they really respect and desire truth and justice, owe it to themselves in turn that they should welcome, and be ready to impartially weigh, Germany's answers to the many malignant misrepresentations to which since August 1914 she has been exposed on the colonial question, as a result of a huge system of propagandism with which she was unable to compete, operating also at a time and in circumstances which made it impossible for her even to obtain a hearing.

It is probable that a large proportion of those who read these pages will have no accurate knowledge, if any knowledge at all, of the way in which the German colonies passed into the present hands. The amazing story will serve as a fitting introduction to the succeeding chapters.

In his Note of November 5, 1918, Robert Lansing, the American Secretary of State, had assured to Germany a just peace based upon President Wilson's Fourteen Points, as these were set forth in the President's "Fourteen Points" speech in Congress on January 8, 1918, and

GERMAN COLONIZATION PAST AND FUTURE

his "Five Points" address of September 27th following, which terms Germany had formally accepted. A contract was thereby established between the Allies on the one hand and the German Empire on the other hand, and this contract clearly defined the fundamental basis of settlement.[1] The question of the German colonies was covered by Point 5, by which the Allies had pledged themselves to abide. The text of Point 5 runs as follows:

> "A free, open-minded and absolutely impartial adjustment of all colonial claims, based upon a strict observance of the principle that in determining all such questions of sovereignty the interests of the populations concerned must have equal weight with the equitable claims of the Government whose title is to be determined."

To what obligations did this stipulation pledge the Allies? In the first place it clearly required them to give Germany a full, fair, and unprejudiced hearing before the fate of her colonies was decided on. The preliminary and essential condition of every just decision is that both sides shall be heard and their claims have judicial consideration. The Allies were, furthermore, bound in fairness to investigate the conditions under which the natives of these colonies lived, and to ascertain their wishes, and that meant an impartial inquiry made by disinterested persons. It is impossible to consider the "interests" of the native populations unless their wishes have first been clearly ascertained. Point 5 guaranteed a free and liberal decision, and this could be achieved only if the decision were based on objective facts instead of, as was actually the case, on agreements for the division of German colonial territory which certain of the Allies *had previously concluded between themselves.*

How did the decision to appropriate the German colonies really come about? For a long time we Germans remained in ignorance of the whole proceedings. The publication of President Wilson's documents, among them extracts from the Protocols of the representative statesmen in whose hands the various decisions lay, at length brought the facts to light. According to these disclosures the forced renunciation of her colonies by Germany was brought about in the following fashion:[2]

On January 13, 1919, the Council of Ten declared itself agreed upon a list of matters which President Wilson had advanced for discussion. In this list the League of Nations occupied the first place, being followed by Reparations and Territorial questions. The question of the German Colonies stood last on the list. In spite of this, on January 23, 1919, Lloyd George proposed that colonial matters should be settled at once, in conjunction with the Eastern Question. Clemenceau, speaking in the name of France, and Sonnino, speaking for Italy, declared themselves agreed, "as though it had all been understood beforehand." Baker writes:

> "Lloyd George, Clemenceau, and Sonnino had long been working together, and knew one another well. They had... negotiated - as we now know more definitely than we did at the time - regarding many of the coming settlements of the peace, both those founded upon the earlier secret treaties and those which had arisen since American interposition in the war had assured ultimate victory to the Allied arms" (vol. i, pp. 251-2).

Wilson resisted, however, declaring that European questions were more pressing. Hereupon the Council of Ten came to the decision that the General Secretary should demand of all delegations of the Powers represented on that body that they should within ten days hand in a declaration of their territorial demands. As Baron Sonnino put it later, *"They wanted to know exactly what they were to get."*

Wilson believed that he had put off the discussion of colonial matters. On the very next day (January 24th), however, Lloyd George again brought up the matter, springing it as a surprise. With an eye to dramatic effect, as Baker remarks, he arranged that the Prime Ministers of the four British Dominions should present themselves together at the French Foreign Office while the Council of Ten was in session. They accordingly appeared, being welcomed by Clemenceau, all according to plan - General Smuts for the South African Union, Borden for Canada, Hughes for Australia, and Massey for New Zealand. Baker writes:

> "They had come to present their claims for the possession of most of the former German colonies which, as Lloyd George explained, had been captured by Dominion troops. Mr. Lloyd George made a brief statement showing that the German colonial policy had been a bad one - 'in South-West Africa they had deliberately pursued a policy of extermination.'"

The Secret Protocol of the Council of Ten contains the following extract regarding the subsequent proceedings:

> "All he (Lloyd George) would like to say on behalf of the British Empire as a whole was that he would be very much opposed to the return to Germany of any of these colonies...
> "President Wilson said that he thought all were agreed to oppose the restoration of the German colonies.
> "M. Orlando, on behalf of Italy, and Baron Makino, on behalf of Japan, agreed.
> "There was no dissentient, and this principle was adopted."[3]

Yet Baker records that the President was "profoundly disturbed" by these proceedings. He writes:

> "It was clear enough that he was to have shrewd opponents - the shrewdest in the world. They were not going to fight him on his main contentions. That would have been poor tactics. It was the familiar policy which he himself described later in the Council of 'acceptance in principle but negation in detail.'
> "In short, after a settlement had been completely made on the order of the old diplomacy and according to the provisions of the

secret treaties, and each nation had got all it could get materially, strategically, and politically, there was to be a pious statement of 'principles leading to justice, morals, and liberty,' and a discussion of the organization of a society of nations."[4]

Thus it was that the appropriation of the German colonies was decided off-hand, without discussion, and without taking the natives, still less Germany, into consideration. Such was the "free, open-minded and absolutely impartial adjustment" promised by Wilson's Fifth Point! Such was the fulfilment of the solemn contract with the German Empire as contained in Lansing's Note of November 5, 1918, so far as Point 5 was concerned!

But the seizure of the German colonies was only one side of the matter. There now arose the question of their division among the Powers which had come into occupation of them in the course of the war. Lloyd George proposed the annexation of the German colonies in the special interest of the British Dominions. "He would like," he said, "the Conference to treat the territories as part of the Dominions which had captured them." And he made this claim in spite of the fact that on January 25, 1918, he had assured the Trade Union leaders, who stood for the "No Annexations" principle: "With regard to the German colonies, I have repeatedly declared that they are held at the disposal of a Conference whose decision must have primary regard to the wishes and interests of the native inhabitants of such colonies."

Wilson declared the solution proposed by Lloyd George to be nothing more than *"a mere distribution of the spoils."* Now the Prime Ministers of the British Dominions presented their claims. Hughes demanded German New Guinea and the German South Sea Islands for Australia; Massey claimed Samoa for New Zealand; and Smuts claimed German South-West Africa for the South African Union. All of them wanted immediate out-and-out annexation and no half-measures. They based their claims upon the expense and losses suffered by the Dominions in the war and the fact that their troops were then occupying the colonies in question, and, further, they called attention to the alleged strategic and military necessities of the Dominions. The interests of the natives, they said, would be secured in the event of annexation, for the Dominions were all democracies, and naturally would do their best for civilization.

On January 27th the representative of Japan, Baron Makino, appeared before the Council of Ten and demanded the absolute surrender to Japan of Kiao-chou and the other rights and privileges of Germany in Shantung, together with the German South Sea Islands north of the Equator. *These demands were based upon a secret agreement concluded between Japan and England in March, 1917* - nearly two years before, while the war was still in progress and its issue uncertain! At that date the Entente had requested Japan's help against the German and Austrian submarines in the Mediterranean, and German territory was to be the payment. The Japanese Government had cautiously stipulated that the cession of these colonies to Japan should be formally guaranteed by treaty.[5] Great Britain had, in fact, promised before this to support Japan's claim to appropriate the German South Sea Islands, and the Anglo-Japanese Agreement on this subject is set forth in the British Note of February 16, 1917.[6] After receiving this assurance, Japan asked France and Russia for their consent. France gave the desired assent on March 1st, but required in return that China should be made to participate in the war against Germany - in other words, that Japan should cease to oppose this idea, as she had previously done. Russia gave her consent shortly before the collapse of the Russian Empire.

France likewise had secret agreements concealed up her sleeve. On January 28, 1919, M. Simon, the French Colonial Minister, demanded the "annexation pure and simple" of Togo and the Cameroons, basing this claim again upon the existence of an understanding with Great Britain. He offered to read two letters exchanged during the war between M. Cambon, French Ambassador to London, and Sir Edward Grey, arranging for the provisional division of these same colonies, but he was promptly headed off by Mr. Lloyd George, who "did not think it would serve any useful purpose to read these documents just then."[7] The exchange of Notes here referred to had taken place on March 24 and May 11, 1916. It was made plain in these Notes that the provisional division of the Cameroons and Togo therein agreed upon between Great Britain and France, for purposes of occupation during the war, should be converted into permanent possession in the event of the Allies at the end of the war securing the right to dispose of these colonies.[8]

Belgium also advanced a claim to a portion of German East Africa. Even Italy made colonial demands on the grounds of the secret Treaty of London concluded with the Entente on April 26, 1915, in which the price of Italy's participation in the war against the Central Powers was fixed. It was declared therein that Italy should receive grants of territory in Africa, should France and Great Britain "extend their colonial possessions in Africa at the expense of Germany."[9]

In the meantime Wilson was called home in February by political exigencies, sailing on the 15th, and Baker writes that in his absence the Council of Ten did its best to wreck the American scheme of peace for the world. He says: "It seemed that every militaristic and nationalistic force came instantly to the fore when Wilson departed."[10]

It is self-evident that all these territorial claims raised by the various Allies on the score of secret treaties were in direct contradiction to Woodrow Wilson's Point 5. The American President perceived and openly declared that the Allies did not concern themselves with the carrying out of his principles, which were to have formed the foundation of the peace as this had been agreed upon. On the contrary, all they cared about was the division of the spoils of war. Nevertheless, in spite of this express conviction, Wilson yielded, permitting the German colonies to be divided up in accordance with these secret treaties, and agreeing that those Powers which had occupied them with their troops should remain in possession. Although his Fifth Point was thus thrown to the winds, he seems to have contented himself with the threadbare reservation that occupation was to be under a system of Mandates, a condition which gave no anxiety to the Powers in possession.

Nevertheless, it is evident that Wilson was never happy about this breach of faith. He had undoubtedly entered on the discussion of the question intending to adhere to his famous Point 5. As late as May 2, 1919, the American Press Bureau stated that though Germany had provisionally been refused any of her colonial possessions, the matter was not as yet definitively settled.

> "Wilson had proposed that she should receive back sufficient colonial territory to make her independent of other countries for tropical raw materials and to provide a sphere for emigration. Germany was, however, to give an undertaking that she would follow no military or political designs in these colonies."

What had been done in January, however, remained. The policy of annexations, formally repudiated by the spokesmen of Great Britain at the beginning of the war, and later by Wilson still more emphatically, prevailed. Even a French journal, *Le Peuple* (May 15, 1919), condemned the arrangement as one under which the territories with their populations were "to change hands just as slaves were of old sold with the other property of their master when he became bankrupt."

Here it should be stated that it was not President Wilson, but General Smuts, the Prime Minister of the South African Union, who invented the Mandate system. Smuts, however, had only proposed that the Turkish possessions to be separated from the Ottoman Empire should be placed under Mandate administration; and he demanded the outright annexation of German South-West Africa by South Africa. What Wilson did was to extend the Mandate system to the German colonies, in order to be able to bring these within the scope of his plans for the League of Nations.

One of the principal participants in the negotiations at Versailles, the American Secretary of State, Lansing, has plainly stated that this procedure of the Allies was not dictated by any consideration for President Wilson's ideas, but by extremely prosaic and egoistic reasoning.

If, it was argued, the German colonies had been so divided between the victorious Powers that each had come into possession of sovereign rights, it would hardly have been possible to avoid reckoning the value of these acquisitions as part of the war tribute to be exacted by them from Germany. Under the system of Mandates, however, the victorious Powers came into possession of Germany's colonial possessions without being obliged to relinquish one tittle of their crushing demands for reparation. As Lansing scathingly puts it:

> "In actual operation the apparent altruism of the mandatory system worked in favour of the selfish and material interests of the Powers which accepted the Mandates.... It should not be a matter of surprise, therefore, that the President found little opposition to the adoption of his theory, or, to be more accurate, of the Smuts theory, on the part of the European statesmen."[11]

The situation was thus brought about that, in spite of the acceptance of the system of Mandates, the Powers severally received exactly that share of the German colonies which they had guaranteed to each other by early secret treaties or later agreements. Great Britain and France divided the West African colonies between them; Japan and Great Britain similarly divided the South Sea Islands; while each of the British Dominions was allowed to keep the colony which it had occupied. The system of the Mandates was only a formality - a mere mask covering the ugly reality. Lansing says:

> "If the advocates of the system intended to avoid through its operation the appearance of taking enemy territory as the spoils of war, it was a subterfuge which deceived no one."[12]

That the subterfuge failed to deceive may be true of the members of the Conference, but the outside world, hardly informed at all of the circumstances, was certainly deceived. Perhaps most people took at their face value the statements that were made as to the institution and ends of Mandate government: they actually believed that it had been deliberately designed in the elevated spirit of philanthropy and humanitarianism as the best way of ensuring the future prosperity and welfare of the native inhabitants of the former German colonies, and that the Powers which had supplanted Germany by the crooked methods described were best fitted to enter upon "the sacred trust of civilization." They believed, too, that these Powers were intended to be only the caretakers for the League of Nations, acting in its name and under its directions, and above all, that it would be a first and fundamental principle of administration in the mandated territories that the military training of the natives would be forbidden, except for police forces and for home defence, so that these wretched people would not again be dragged into wars between European nations - a calamity which, as will be shown, Germany strove to prevent in 1914.

Doubts upon these points should have been aroused in the minds of any persons who had even a rudimentary knowledge of colonial matters when the Belgians and the French were chosen as Mandatories. For the world has not yet forgotten the story of the Belgian Congo atrocities, nor of those which followed in the French Congo on the Belgian model. It is also a well-known fact that it is precisely France which pursues a systematic plan of militarizing the natives within her colonial empire and training them for warlike purposes in any part of the world to which she chooses to send them.

It is unfortunate, however, that the great mass of people in all countries are still too little informed about colonial affairs to be able to submit to the test of fact and truth the specious and one-sided statements put forward for their consumption by leading statesmen of the Allies and the section of the Press at their command. The public has heard much of the idealistic motives and moral considerations which are alleged to have determined the action of the Powers which have taken the German colonies, but little or nothing of the way in which this bartering of territory and population was actually carried out. It is just from the *moral point of view* that the episode presents so unpleasant and sinister an aspect. For it was only when a prearranged plan for the dividing up of the German colonies had to be defended before the world that the Allied Governments began to talk of morality and to profess that they were concerned only for the good of the natives.

Thus it is that the action of the Allies in this matter involves a threefold deception.

(1) The first deception was practised upon the German nation. By deluding the German people with the promise of peace based upon President Wilson's Fourteen Points, the Allies led them to believe that the colonial question would be subjected to "free, open-minded, and absolutely impartial adjustment." Instead of this, the German colonies were arbitrarily confiscated in virtue of military predominance, in anticipation, if not in fact, while the war was still in progress, in virtue of secret agreements concluded before the Lansing Note laid down the principles of the peace to which America and her Allies nevertheless solemnly pledged themselves!

(2) The native populations of the German colonies were also the victims of deception. The Allies had raised a great hue and cry about the right of the peoples to "self-determination." Lloyd George repeatedly declared in public that the native chiefs and tribes would be consulted before a mandate over a former German colony would be granted to any nation. This, again, proved to be nothing more than a blind. In reality, the partition took place without the wishes of the natives being seriously considered at all. It will also be proved that native interests have not only been neglected, but in some instances have even been seriously injured by the change.

(3) Finally, the public has been grossly deceived. Every possible attempt was made to create the impression that the decision respecting

the fate of the German colonies was arrived at only in accordance with ethical principles. Although secret treaties formally providing for their partition had already been concluded, the final act was cloked with moral professions, and the world was told that the object in view was to secure for the native populations better conditions than had been theirs under German rule. In effect, however, the Allies in conclave divided territory and drew new frontier lines in the most arbitrary fashion without any regard for the natural boundaries of the tribes, and never even tried to keep up the fiction of the "self-determination" of the peoples. Yet while the military and economic interests of the participating States were the only factors really considered in seizing Germany's colonial possessions, the world was asked to believe that they were fulfilling "a sacred trust of civilization."

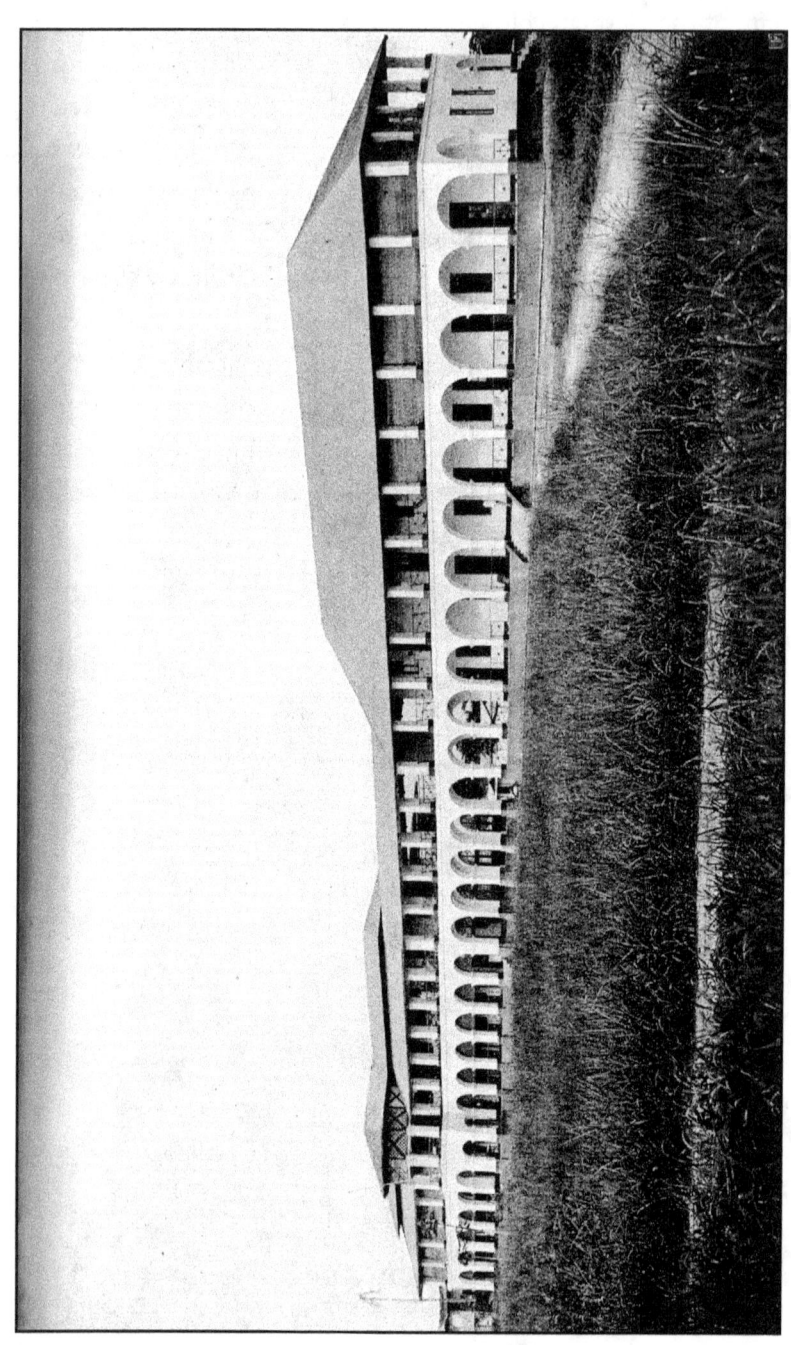
Government Hospital, Duala, The Cameroons

Native Hospital, Duala, The Cameroons

4

The Myth of German "Colonial Guilt"

It is necessary to examine closely the claim of the Allied Powers that only they, and not Germany, can be trusted to administer colonial territories efficiently and for the good of their native populations. Only then will the reader be enabled to perceive clearly the hollowness of the pretences under which Germany has been deprived of territories every one of which she held by a tenure as rightful and honest as any claimed by the Allied Powers, with the additional force that her title to nearly all of them was at one time or another formally recognized by treaty by one or other, and in some cases several, of the very Powers which have now seized them as a prize of war.

Take first the interests of the native populations. If Germany had really treated her natives as badly as the world was so often told after the war, had she really been guilty of such sins of omission and commission as she is charged with in the Notes to the Treaty of Versailles and other official pronouncements of the Entente, then the fact must have become evident before the war in the reports of foreign observers. Foreign criticism is not accustomed, in the case of real atrocities on a systematic scale, to be particularly reticent or indulgent. Yet there existed nowhere in the world any evidence of disapproval or even suspicion of German methods of colonization such as that which was justifiably advanced against French and Belgian methods before the war. In reading the reports of foreign colonial experts and travellers upon the German colonies, we do not encounter a single accusation of that kind. On the contrary, there are many tributes to German colonial activity and success. The unprejudiced reader will find it interesting to read a few that are characteristic out of the great mass available. It will be seen that most of them relate to the years immediately preceding the war - in other words, to the conditions which have been misrepresented by our enemies for war and other political purposes.[1]

During a meeting of the Royal Colonial Institute held on January 13, 1914, the late Viscount Milner, the chairman (who as an ex-High Commissioner for South Africa must have known well German South-West Africa and how it was governed), following a lecture by a German professor, remarked:

> "Great Britain has had a long and very diversified experience as a colonizing country. Germany is a comparative new-comer in the colonial field, but having entered, she has thrown herself into the unfamiliar task with characteristic thoroughness and energy. It would be a great mistake to think that we have nothing to learn from her experience in that field, as she admittedly has much to learn - something, at any rate - from our long history as a colonizing people."

On the same occasion, Mr. George Foster, M. P., Canadian Minister of Commerce, stated:

> "The vigour and strength and system with which Germany, not to mention other European countries, has of late years thrown herself into the work of outside colonization, has been very marked and notable."

Sir Charles Eliot, Royal Commissioner for British East Africa from 1901 to 1904, writes as follows in his book *The East African Protectorate* (1905) of the work achieved in the adjacent German colony:

> "As might be expected, the scientific departments, which have been almost entirely neglected in the British possessions, have received great attention.... The Germans are said to deal with natives more severely than we do, and to be less popular with them.... On the other hand, natives are said to immigrate into German territory from the Congo Free State and the Portuguese dominions, so that they cannot find the *régime* very distasteful."

In the same book Eliot says: "I would not have us lay any flattering unction to our souls, and congratulate ourselves, as we are wont to do, on managing everything better than all other nations."

Only two years before the war, the Rev. J. H. Harris, in his book *Dawn in Darkest Africa* (1912), advocated the increase of Germany's colonial stake in Africa, proposing the transference to her of the Upper Congo and the Belgian Congo. He wrote:

> "Great Britain has a full share of responsibilities in the African continent. France, Belgium, and Portugal, even if they desired to enlarge their tropical dependencies, have not yet established a case for expansion. Quite the reverse. One Power alone - Germany - is not only capable but apparently desirous of adding to her colonial possessions... (p. 301).
>
> "If France and Belgium together could be persuaded to transfer the whole or the greater part of French and Belgian Congo to Germany,... they would individually be immeasurably the gainers, they would secure the peace of the world, and they would thereby add a lustre to their names which neither time nor eternity could tarnish.

GERMAN COLONIZATION PAST AND FUTURE

> "German administration of French Congo certainly could hardly be more oppressive than the French Government permits to-day. In Belgian Congo the natives would probably be treated as humanely and probably more justly than at present.... On the whole, both from the commercial and native standpoint, the Congo Basin stands to gain by a transfer to the German Empire" (p. 303).

His idea was that Belgium should be paid in cash, and that in favour of France there should be a rectification of the frontier of Alsace-Lorraine, or the "lost provinces" be given complete autonomy.

Again, in the English magazine *United Empire* for July, 1913, is an article on the German colonies by L. Hamilton, who states:

> "Wherever the German may be, the schoolmaster is abroad. With the missionaries, the colonial Governments have developed education to quite an astonishing extent."

Two English officials from Northern Rhodesia, by name Frank H. Melland and Edward H. Cholmely, travelled through German East Africa, and published their impressions in a book called *Through the Heart of Africa* (London, 1912), and these are the conclusions to which they came:

> "The common impression that we should not find much to learn from the German administration of East Africa is founded on a superficial or out-of-date knowledge of the facts.... Naturally enough, we judged the German system by our own, and in some ways found it wanting; as a nation we have had far greater experience in ruling tropical countries, and we were quick to notice what we considered to be weak points in the German administration; but at the same time we saw much to admire, and the general verdict must, we think, be one of congratulation to our

neighbours (p. 93).... On the whole, considering how new colonial work is to the German nation, they have every reason to be proud of what they are doing in their East African Protectorate" (p. 101).

I may also cite two American judgments. Theodore Roosevelt, the former President of the United States, wrote as follows in his book *African Game Trails* (1910), dealing with his African experiences in regard to the German planters, Government officials, and officers:

> "They are first-class men, these English and Germans; both are doing in East Africa a work of worth to the whole world; there is ample room for both, and no possible cause for any but a thoroughly friendly rivalry" (p. 5).

Another American traveller, E. A. Forbes, who spent a considerable time in Africa, wrote in the *American Review of Reviews* in 1911:

> "Of all the overlords of Africa the German has the cleanest hands and the best prospects. His African invasion was characterized by the most artful diplomacy, but even his bitterest enemy could scarcely declare that he did not play fair.
>
> "I have closely observed the Germans in their intercourse with their half-savage *protégés* on the West Coast. Administration and government on the black continent are largely a question of temperament, and to all appearances the Germans are less liable to give way to irritation and excitement than other white men. I have studied all the white races engaged in the work of awakening Africa, and I cannot avoid the conviction that the German native will develop himself as highly as all the others, if, indeed, not more highly."

Moreover, if German colonial activities had been so pernicious as they are represented to be in the Versailles Treaty and the accompanying documents, how can be explained the fact that shortly before the war the British Government was about to sign treaties with Germany which would have ceded to her further tracts of colonial territory? Long negotiations had then resulted in the drawing up of an Anglo-German treaty in which Germany was promised a large share of the Portuguese possessions in Africa in the event of Portugal being disposed, for financial reasons, to give up these colonies, and even boundary adjustments which would have handed over British territory to her. If Germany's administration of her colonies had really been such as to make it impossible ever again to place the responsibility for the training of natives into her hands - as the Mantle Note of July 16, 1919, declared - then the conduct of Great Britain in proposing to hand over numerous native tribes to Germany in this pre-war colonial agreement would have been inexplicable. There is only one explanation, and it is quite simple. The propagandism about Germany's alleged evil colonial record was organized, and in large part invented, without the slightest regard for logic or consistency, for the one purpose of covering with the cloke of righteousness an indefensible act of sheer cupidity.

The fable of Germany's "colonial guilt" was built up during the World War. Never before had it been breathed. At first there was a private agitation on a small scale, demanding the seizure of Germany's colonies, and combining this demand with attacks upon Germany's colonial policy. This agitation began in the early stages of the war, but met at first with no official encouragement. In 1917, however, when the entry of the United States into the war had brought the prospect of final victory within sight, the British Government came out in the open with public statements purporting to prepare the public mind for the seizure of the German colonies and to justify this by discrediting German colonial administration. In March, 1917, a special "commission" composed of scientists and other experts was appointed, to prepare the material for the British delegates to the future Peace Conference. It was this commission which mobilized the attacks against the German colonial administration.

In July, 1918, when as a result of the counter-offensive of the Entente Powers the fortunes of war seemed to be turning definitely against Germany, official Great Britain began to take a firm stand on the colonial question. Finally, when the Versailles Treaty was forced upon Germany, the alleged maladministration of her colonies was used as a pretext wherewith to quieten the scruples of those who had been assured, and who still believed, that England did not go to war for the acquisition of more territory. This cursory historical survey suffices to show clearly that the fiction of Germany's colonial incapacity was concocted, developed, and spread abroad merely as a convenient means of effecting certain definite political ends which had been decided upon in secret long before.

As soon as the machinery of propagandism was well in motion the myth of Germany's "colonial guilt" was disseminated in a vast number of official and unofficial speeches, pamphlets, newspaper articles, etc. The concentrated expression of this false witness is to be found in the Allied Note of June 16, 1919, which contains a reply to the comments of the German delegates upon the terms of peace and at the same time an ultimatum, demanding the signing of the peace treaty by the German Government within five days, and in the covering Note, in which the alleged justification for the conditions of peace, as arbitrarily settled by the Allies, is stated.

The reasons for the seizure of the German colonial possessions are set forth as follows in the Note addressed to the President of the German Delegation covering the reply of the Allied and Associated Powers:

> "Finally, the Allied and Associated Powers are satisfied that the native inhabitants of the German colonies are strongly opposed to being again brought under Germany's sway, and the record of German rule, the traditions of the German Government, and

the use to which these colonies were put as bases from which to prey upon the commerce of the world, make it impossible for the Allied and Associated Powers to return them to Germany, or to entrust to her the responsibility for the training and education of their inhabitants."

In the reply of the Allied and Associated Powers itself there occurs the following passage:

"In requiring Germany to renounce all her rights and claims to her overseas possessions, the Allied and Associated Powers placed before every other consideration the interests of the native populations advocated by President Wilson in the Fifth Point of his Fourteen Points mentioned in his address of the 8th January, 1918. Reference to the evidence from German sources previous to the war of an official as well as of a private character, and to the formal charges made in the Reichstag, especially by MM. Erzberger and Noske, will suffice to throw full light upon the German colonial administration, upon the cruel methods of repression, the arbitrary requisitions, and the various forms of forced labour which resulted in the depopulation of vast expanses of territory in German East Africa and the Cameroons, not to mention the tragic fate of the Hereros in South-West Africa, which is well known to all.

"Germany's dereliction in the sphere of colonial civilization has been revealed too completely to admit of the Allied and Associated Powers consenting to make a second experiment and of their assuming the responsibility of again abandoning thirteen or fourteen millions of natives to a fate from which the war has delivered them.

"Moreover, the Allied and Associated Powers felt themselves compelled to safeguard their own security and the peace of the world against a military imperialism which sought to establish bases whence it could pursue a policy of interference and intimidation against the other Powers."

Where did the authors of these Notes acquire their knowledge of colonial matters? It is well known that the author of the covering Note, which bore the signature of Clemenceau when delivered to the German Government, was in reality written by an official in the service of Mr. Lloyd George. It is natural, therefore, that he should have obtained his material from English sources, and indeed the very wording of the Reply Note shows clearly that it was founded upon English material. The principal basis for the statements contained in the Notes is obviously the industrious and exhaustive work of the special commission above named, which, as I have said, began as early as March, 1917, under the direction of the British Foreign Office, to prepare the material for the British delegates to the peace negotiations. The Handbooks which were compiled by this commission and utilized at the Peace Conference were published in 1920.[2]

The Handbooks on the German colonies are not by any means uniform in contents and tendency. Some, mainly objective and scientific, confine themselves to giving a description of the geographical conditions, history, and economical development of the territories, whilst others, especially that entitled *Treatment of Natives in the German Colonies,* are malicious and slanderous compilations of everything prejudicial which has ever been said of German colonization, *without a single reference to the generous and impartial testimony abundantly volunteered by English and other foreign observers in praise of German colonization and administration.* Such dishonourable methods of propagandism are entirely unworthy of the reputation for fair-play which Englishmen have claimed in the past, and which many people of other nations have hitherto been ready to acknowledge.

In order to characterize the spirit of these writings, it is only necessary to examine the evidence upon which they were based. Every question asked or accusation levelled in the German Parliament at the time of the "colonial scandals" against this or that colonial official, however far in the past, is carefully noted, *but the answers to these questions are never given, nor are the results of the investigations or the judgments of absolutely impartial German judges, which usually resulted in the refutation of the accusations.* It is impossible that the assiduous compilers should have been ignorant of these results, for such an assumption would stamp them as incompetent as well as malicious, since the result of every investigation was laid before the Reichstag in a memorial. No, what they did was to mass together all the accusations they could lay hold of, however baseless and fraudulent, and to hush up official replies, disclaimers, and disproofs. The result of this discreditable procedure is that the reader, ignorant of the truth, imagines that he is reading a complete record of proved facts, instead of a selected and biassed compilation of unproved accusations by members of the Reichstag, principally Socialists, who, like most English Socialists, are inclined to regard all European colonization among coloured people as a reprehensible form of profiteering.

In addition to this, the utterances of German parliamentarians are often deliberately torn from their context. The same member frequently combined with his accusations something greatly to the credit of German colonization, *but this part of his speech is invariably suppressed.* As an example let me mention the case of the well-known member of the Catholic or Centre Party, the late Matthias Erzberger. As a free-lance journalist, not over-popular in his own party, Erzberger levelled at one time or another many sharp criticisms at German colonial policy, some of which were totally unjustified, and he is cited in the Entente Note to the Versailles Treaty as the principal witness for the evils of German colonial methods. The accusations levelled by Erzberger against the Government are reported in full. *But all the good which Erzberger said of German colonial policy, and in particular his warm praise of the policy pursued with regard to the natives in German East Africa, is absolutely ignored and omitted* (cf. speech in the Reichstag, February 27, 1918).

It is also a fact that one of the most powerful defences of Germany as a colonial Power, one of the most indignant refutations of the false accusations of her critics, came from the pen of the same Erzberger, *but no mention of this fact will be found in any British propagandist publication.*

The second principal witness cited in the Entente Note, Gustav Noske, a Social-Democratic member of the Reichstag, also repeatedly criticized the abuses which, *according to Socialistic conceptions,* occurred in the colonies. On the other hand, in a book which he published in May, 1914 (i.e. before the war), under the title *Colonial Policy and Social Democracy,* after mentioning what, according to his ideas, was still capable of improvement in the colonies, he brought forward a considerable body of material to show how a most reasonable spirit was gradually making itself felt in German colonial policy. As was to be expected, the English propaganda pamphlets which made use of Noske's attacks *suppressed these favourable passages.*

In view of all that has been said, it is hardly needful to repeat that the propagandist Handbooks were composed solely in order to provide a moral pretext for the intended seizure of the German colonies. The impression left on the mind of the uninformed English reader is that the existing conditions in the German colonies approximated to the atrocities which were branded before the world in the case of the Belgian and French Congo territories, and to inspire in him the desire that the unfortunate blacks should be liberated from a similar horrible fate. The misrepresentations, of course, adopt the air of being objective and scientific. It is, therefore, quite possible that some members of a delegation at Versailles were equally convinced that it would be a blessing to liberate the natives from the German yoke.

The attacks against German colonization in German South-West Africa were separately prepared in the form of a British Blue Book entitled *Report on the Natives of South-West Africa and their Treatment by Germany* (London, 1918). A publication called *German Colonisers in Africa,* written by one Evans Lewin and published in German at Zurich

GERMAN COLONIZATION PAST AND FUTURE

in 1918, played a large part in this propagandism, and it seems also to have furnished the authors of some of the Handbooks already mentioned with material. In this slanderous pamphlet we find the author using, with execrable taste, comparisons out of the Old Testament in order to disparage German colonization. He stigmatizes the German colonists - all of them - as "cruel, brutal, arrogant and wholly unsuited for intercourse with primitive peoples," and "lustful and malicious in their moral attitude to subject races."

The author of this pamphlet, by perversions of the truth, by generalizations of single incidents, and by citing detached parts of speeches and opinions of members of the Reichstag, missionaries, etc., succeeds in constructing a horrible picture, but it is a base caricature of the facts. Most of the parliamentarians and missionaries whom he misquoted issued a public protest against his abuse of their words, and published them in their proper connexion in a pamphlet which was issued in Basle in 1918, with the title *German Colonial Policy before the Tribunal of the World*. Pater van der Burgt, a Dutch missionary, who had been cited by Lewin as a neutral witness, likewise repudiated his assertions in the *Koloniale Rundschau* in 1919. Nevertheless, I have been unable to discover that any notice whatever was taken of these corrections in later literature, and it is justifiable to believe that they were ignored in the same methodical way that the truth was ignored in the original publications.

Lewin's slanderous publication also makes use of an *Open Letter* published by Bishop Frank Weston, leader of the English University Mission in Zanzibar and East Africa, in which the principal charge made against the Germans is the introduction of forced labour. It would be interesting to know whether this *Open Letter* was written without prior arrangement with, or at least without the prior knowledge of, General Smuts, who was bent on annexing German South-West.

I do not suggest for a moment that Bishop Weston, in publishing his temperamental and exaggerated statement, acted in bad faith, yet the fact remains that before the war he lived in the friendliest relations with the German authorities in East Africa and, so far as I am aware, had no grievance to bring against German administration. A German Protestant missionary, Dr. A. W. Schreiber, criticizing the Weston attacks, has written:

> "If the treatment of the natives was in Bishop Weston's opinion as scandalous as he represents, why did this humane man - to whom the ear of the Government and of every District Administrator, and also the columns of the Press, were as open as to others - maintain complete silence until his proof of these alleged excesses could be used for the purpose of transferring German East Africa into British possession? We missionaries have always waged unrelenting warfare against the abuse of the whip, and we always shall do. But we found ample reason for so doing in British possessions likewise."[3]

There for the moment I leave the matter, only asking the reader to consider what would be said of Bishop Weston's evidence in a court of law in the circumstances above stated.

Maternity Hospital at Windhoek, South-West Africa

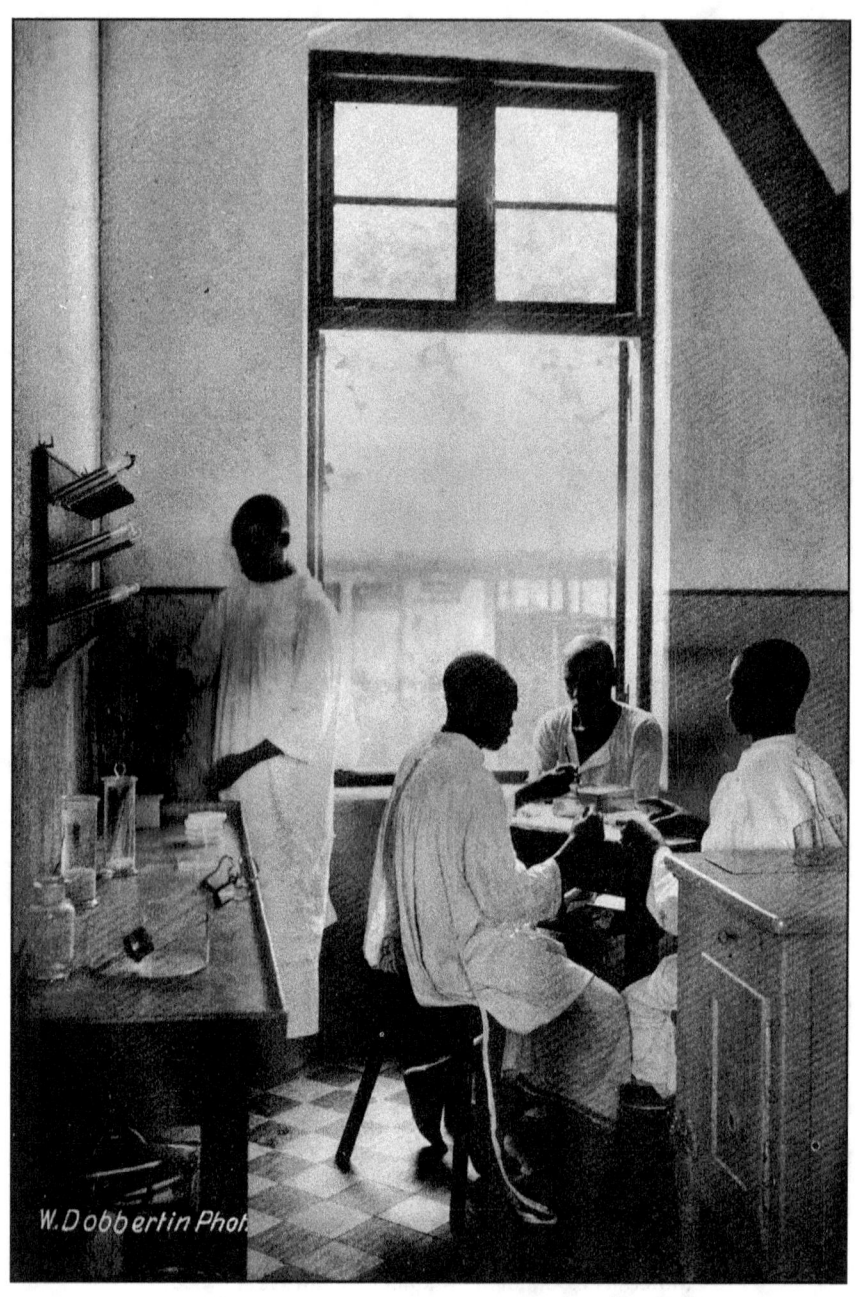
Native laboratory assistants in the Institution for Epidemic Research, Dar-es-Salam, German East Africa

5

The Alleged Militarism in the German Colonies

Having exposed the methods of the anti-German propagandists, it is time to survey more particularly the substance of their charges. Two charges which have been systematically drummed into the ears of the world, and particularly neutral nations, are that Germany had militarized her colonies, had used them as "bases from which to prey upon the commerce of the world," and to menace other nations - this absurd charge is made in Reply Note of the Allied Powers to Germany's representations on the Versailles Treaty - and that she had systematically ill-treated the native populations under her rule.

I. The Charge of Militarism Examined

Taking these charges in order, I assert without hesitation that there never was the slightest foundation for the myth of an aggressive Germany desirous of acquiring territories overseas in order to use them for the injury of other Powers. This fact is so obvious that it would not have needed statement were it not that the continual denial of it has become a source of so much misrepresentation. As an instance of how the scales of justice were weighed against Germany during the war by men who wanted to get hold of her oversea possessions, I may recall an article published by Mr. Massey, the Prime Minister of New Zealand, wherein he wrote:

> "It is important to remember that commercial development was not Germany's primary aim when she acquired her possessions in the Pacific. The evidence is now indisputable that her first and main object was to secure strong naval bases, from which, in the event of war, her cruisers and submarines would be able to dominate and raid the great ocean highways to the Far East and to Australia and New Zealand."

Now Germany obtained nearly all her colonies in 1884-5. The suggestion that it was her ruling design "from the first" to make them bases for submarine warfare *at a time when submarines were hardly heard of,* and many years before their utility in warfare became recognized - first by France and England - is a proof not so much of ignorance in the writer, who knew better, but of an attempt to impose on the ignorance and credulity of the uninformed multitude. The fact is that the first British submarines were launched early in 1901, while the German Naval Estimates contained a vote for submarines for the first time in 1905, and then it was for the bagatelle of £75,000, and was for "experiments."

The interests of historical truth, if nothing else, demand that this accusation of aggressive purpose be refuted as in direct contradiction to the facts. Such points of vantage for military purposes never existed in the German colonies, neither were any planned or contemplated. The one apparent exception is the naval station of Tsing-tao (Kiao-chou), which was made an armed post just as the British position at Wei-Hai-Wei was, and for the same reason of self-defence. For the rest, there were in the German protectorates no fortified naval stations (though both Great Britain and France had many formidable ones), no harbours for U-boats, and none from which the submarines, had such existed, could have sallied forth. There were no harbour fortifications, no shore batteries, under shelter of which German war-vessels could have held themselves in readiness, no places in which they could have lain in safety and taken in coal. There was nothing of this kind. Such enterprises would have necessitated the stationing of a considerable number of warships in the African and South Sea colonies, but this was never done. One small cruiser was stationed off German East Africa; but as a rule there were either no ships at all stationed at the other colonies, or only antiquated warships, with guns of small calibre.

When the war broke out the few small warships which did happen to be in the neighbourhood of the German colonies in Africa and the South Sea were compelled to leave the harbours of the Protectorates concerned, because these could offer them no protection. Naturally, they received orders from the Admiralty at home to pursue cruiser warfare, so far as they were at all capable of being used for such a purpose, but precisely because of Germany's great lack of colonial naval stations they were forced to take in coal and other necessities as opportunity provided on the high seas. The cruiser *Königsberg*, which had been stationed in East Africa, finding the provisioning on the high seas no longer possible in spite of splendid leadership and achievements, and being utterly without any fortified point of support on the East African coast, was only able to take cover by running in at the mouth of the Rufiji River, which had been held by the enemy to be unnavigable.

Even such a bare possibility as this did not exist in the other African and South Sea colonies. The German harbours and coast towns lay unprotected and exposed to the cannon of the enemy's warships. Dar-es-Salam, the principal harbour in German East Africa, our largest colony, boasted only a few old saluting guns, fired with powder which developed clouds of smoke. Duala, in the Cameroons, was similarly equipped. Not a single other harbour in the African or any of the other colonies possessed cannon of any sort. Here and there attempts were made to block the harbour mouths by sinking ships or other methods, but these were mere improvisations, primitive methods of self-help.

Nothing was prepared even for defence against an attack by sea, much less for the setting up of "points of support for an aggressive policy" on the part of German warships. In view of these facts it is an ungenerous and unchivalrous misuse of language to talk of the German colonies being used as starting-points for commercial piracy.

One thing more I would add: every penny expended on our colonies, whether derived from the German treasury or the independent revenues of the Protectorates, had to be accounted for to the Reichstag, and the records of parliamentary discussions will be sought in vain for any speech, statement, or other evidence countenancing in any way this absurd yet malicious accusation. No critics of colonial policy in general were so unsparing as the Social Democrats, simply because they disapproved of colonies, in accordance with the traditional principles of their party. Can anyone doubt that if the accusation had at any time had even the appearance of reality these lynx-eyed critics would not have exploited it for all it and they were worth?

Let the reader judge fairly and impartially, for he owes it to himself so to do. If the conquest of oversea possessions by force of arms be taken as the proof of a militaristic imperialism on the part of a nation or its Government, then Germany need not plead guilty. Great Britain and France, however, both followed an active and militant policy of imperialism during the period in question. But if such action be not the test and proof of militant imperialism, how can Germany be held to have displayed such imperialism in the colonies? In the twenty-four years from the fall of Bismarck to the World War, Germany had sought and achieved very little in the sphere of colonial expansion. She acquired only Kiao-chou in China,[1] the little South Sea Island of Samoa, the Caroline Islands (these by purchase), the Marianne Islands, and last of all, the extreme corner of the Congo as an expansion of the West African colony of the Cameroons. These were not spoils of war, but the result of peaceful treaties, which cannot be said of all the territorial acquisitions effected during the same period by the Allied Powers.

These extensions of Germany's colonial possessions during the reign of William II shrink into insignificance when compared with the British and French colonial expansion during the same period. Great Britain not only annexed the Boer Republics as the result of the Transvaal War, but secured possession of Egypt and the reconquered Soudan, and made other extensive additions to her African empire. She also extended her colonial possessions by the occupation of Wei-Hai-Wei in Eastern Asia, and the acquisition of the Tonga Islands and some of the Solomon Islands.

France since 1890 has acquired still vaster stretches of colonial territory than Great Britain, for the greater part of her enormous colonial empire in Africa was annexed during that period. Warlike expeditions against the natives played a great part in these acquisitions. During the two decades preceding the World War, the French possessions in Asia were also considerably enlarged. Indeed, more than once France, in pursuing her aggressive policy in both continents, narrowly escaped coming into violent conflict with Great Britain. It is only necessary to recall the Siamese and Fashoda episodes.

In the entire scheme of German colonial policy there is nothing which could justify the accusation of aggression, and those who make it are bound in honour to prove it, which they have never done. Far from being aggressive and egoistic in colonial matters, Germany let slip many an opportunity which presented itself for the increase of her colonial possessions by special treaties with other Powers. Bismarck's successor, Count Caprivi, was disinclined to increase Germany's colonial dominion, and gave up great tracts of East African territory in exchange for Heligoland. The later Chancellor, Prince Bülow, who remained in office for so many years, set up as a motto of German policy: "No conquests, no fresh territorial acquisitions, but in place of these the continuance of the policy of the Open Door." When the Morocco affair made the continuance of this policy impossible in consequence of France's imperialistic attitude, in which she was supported by Great Britain, whose *quid pro quo* was a free hand in Egypt, Kiderlen-Waechter allowed himself to be persuaded to recognize France's claims to complete her domination in North Africa - the unhappy results of which are only now maturing - in return for a little West African territory of small importance ceded from the French Congo. The land in question was primeval forest, totally uncultivated, and could not be made to serve as a military station for the terrorizing of other Powers, or France assuredly would have been unwilling to part with it. An Anglo-German treaty, which was agreed upon immediately before the war, had for its object the peaceful penetration of a part of the Portuguese possessions by means of German colonization. Germany was later to buy these lands from Portugal should financial considerations incline her to the sale, while Great Britain was to exercise the same right in respect of Mozambique. This arrangement hardly comes under the heading of imperialistic militarism. If it does, how stands it with Germany's partner to the bargain?[2]

I come now to the alleged militarization of the natives in the German colonies themselves. Merely to mention the legal restrictions as to the number of the colonial troops should be a sufficient refutation of this accusation. Only the three largest colonies - German East Africa, German South-West Africa, and the Cameroons - possessed Protectorate troops which were even organized as military troops. The Protectorate Troops Law of July 7-18, 1896, defines clearly enough the purpose of this force. It might only be used for the maintenance of public order and security in the African Protectorate territories, and the very number of these troops shows clearly that they could have been used for no other purpose.[3] German East Africa, which has an area about twice as large as that of the German Empire, with approximately seven and three-quarter million black natives, possessed a Protectorate force of 2,500 native soldiers, commanded by 152 German officers and sub-officers, exclusive of 108 German Red Cross officers and sub-officers. In addition there was a police force composed of 2,140 coloured natives, under four German officers and 61 sub-officers, which served for purely police duties. Up to the outbreak of the World War these troops were armed with old rifles, single-shot guns, which used a powder producing much smoke.

It is obvious that such weapons could only be used in defensive action against natives, and would be worthless if employed against armies armed with modern repeating rifles and smokeless powder; although in the neighbouring British and Belgian colonies the coloured troops were armed with such modern weapons even before the war. German East Africa followed this example very slowly, and when the war broke out was just beginning to introduce modern weapons into a few companies. There was no artillery at all, with the exception of the old salute guns before mentioned and a few very small cannon, intended purely for use in the event of warfare with the natives.

Conditions in the Cameroons were much the same, with the exception that the numbers of Protectorate troops and police were far smaller than in East Africa. There were there 1,550 native troops and 1,285 native police, with the corresponding number of German officers and sub-officers.

German South-West Africa was the only colony which possessed a body of white Protectorate troops, and it numbered less than 2,000. The white police force was a body of between 500 and 600 men. It is obvious that this small body of troops and police, in charge of a territory more than half as large again as Germany, could only be intended to serve the purpose of maintaining order in regions not very thickly populated but whose population consisted of natives of very uncertain temper, as the South African Union authorities have since discovered.

The other German colonies possessed no Protectorate troops at all, but small police forces. These forces consisted in Togo of 500 natives and in German New Guinea, including the scattered islands, of 830 natives. In Samoa there was only a small police force composed of about thirty sons of native chieftains, and it served purely decorative purposes. This body was called the *Fitafita*.

The small number of troops in the German colonies can leave in reasonable minds no doubt of the fact that they can only have been intended to uphold order and security in the country itself, and that is how they were in fact used. This is particularly evident when their numbers are compared with those in neighbouring colonial territories. The German Protectorate and police troops were kept within the limits of what was usual in British colonies under similar conditions, and remained considerably below the number of such forces in French and Belgian territory.

In this connexion it should not be forgotten that in case of a serious insurrection England was in a position to draw upon her Indian troops, and did so on various occasions in British East Africa, whereas Germany had no such reserves. No impartial judge, familiar with conditions in such colonial territories, could say that the troops in the German Protectorates were more numerous than was necessary for creating and upholding order and for assuring the undisturbed development of the countries affected.

In regard to East Africa, this is confirmed by an English authority, Brigadier-General C. P. Fendall, who writes in *The East African Force, 1915 - 1919* (1921):

> "There was an idea that should war break out between England and Germany there would be no active fighting in Africa.... It was feared that the prestige of the white man would be lowered, and that the progress of civilization in Africa would be put back a hundred years. The prevalence of this idea led to the maintenance, both in British and German East Africa, of *only sufficient troops to deal with local risings"* (pp. 22-3).

The idea that the Germans might have used these small bodies of isolated troops, which in the event of war would at once have been cut off from all supplies from home, for the purposes of conquering neighbouring territory, is supremely ridiculous. Not a soul, either in Germany or in the German colonies, ever conceived of such an act of insanity.

Had aggressive plans of the kind existed, it would have been necessary to create far larger bodies of troops and to have equipped them with modern weapons as well as with artillery and depots of arms and ammunition. Yet when the World War came, and was carried into the German colonies in direct violation of the White Man's Pact - the Congo Act of 1885 - there was a sufficiency neither of troops, arms, nor ammunition in the German Protectorates to offer successful and continued resistance to an enemy who was vastly superior in numbers and equipment, and who came crowding in on all sides. The fact that so much was nevertheless achieved, and that the main body of the German East African troops in particular were able to maintain themselves in the field during the entire war, was due not only to the excellence of German leadership and the support which the coloured troops received through the enrolment of German reservists, but also to the fidelity of the natives themselves. To this point, however, it will be necessary to return later.

The facts stated should be sufficient to show the groundlessness of the charge of militarization of the German colonies. Comparison of the German with the French military system can only serve to make a clear case clearer still. Germany had *no colonial army, no coloured troops outside the colonies, no conscription of coloured troops* - in fact, no plans or arrangements at all for the utilization of the blacks other than to uphold order and security in their own territories. On the other hand, what is the picture presented by the French colonies? It is a well-known fact that the French militarize their colonies to the greatest possible extent. Every male native of these colonies is liable to serve in the French army and to fight for France wherever it may suit her needs or interests to send him. It is in order that this liability may be imposed on the millions of her helpless natives, and not from any respect for the principles of equality and fraternity as between white and black, that the French make their oversea colonies integral "provinces" of France, since thereby the whole of the French dominions form a single political unit.

And what is the effect of this cruel and immoral system? Can it be that the British, with their world-wide Empire, are happy or proud in the knowledge that during the late war their Ally poured nearly a million coloured soldiers into the field to fight against Europeans? By so doing France has set an example of evil and sinister significance, as a consequence of which the entire attitude of the native races towards the whites has been changed vastly for the worse, their old respect and deference for the European have been diminished or altogether dispelled, and the native everywhere has been taught to regard himself as the equal, if not the superior, of those whom he had been accustomed to look up to as his masters, since he finds that they cannot now carry on their wars with each other without his help.

Since the end of the war France has called more and more of her coloured subjects, especially her African negroes, into military service. According to the *Dépêche Coloniale et Maritime* for January, 1925, there were early in this year 200,000 regular coloured soldiers in the French army, of whom about 100,000 were brown North Africans, 75,000 negroes from Central Africa and elsewhere, and the rest mainly Asiatics from Indo-China. It is also reported that the number is to be increased to 300,000, and this, bear in mind, in time of peace. Military barracks filled with coloured troops are now found in all parts of France, as well as, unhappily, in the western part of my own country. Reflective people hardly need to be told what a potentiality of evil is here represented. This wholesale drafting into the French army of native and coloured people is done so that the thinly flowing blood of the mother country may be conserved. American and European newspaper correspondents in Morocco and Syria have written that only a comparatively small proportion of the French troops engaged in those countries are poilus. A French Army Order of February 21, 1922 *(Bulletin officiel du Ministère des Colonies, 22 Mars, 1922, No. 3),* expressly declares that all natives called up to military service may be used outside their native colony, except in certain clearly defined cases, such as physical unfitness, approaching expiry of period of service, etc.

And how do the natives under French rule like being militarized, and what is the effect upon them? The *Dépêche Coloniale et Maritime* of February 16, 1922, contains the following remarks upon this point by M. Delafosse:

> "Whether we like it or not, we are constrained to admit the fact that recruiting is generally unpopular in our colonies. During and since the war we have certainly succeeded, as a result of persistent efforts, in enlisting large numbers of natives; but in how many cases was the recruit really a volunteer? In certain districts, it is true, there were numbers of young folk who allowed themselves to be enlisted without complaint, and even some who came and enlisted voluntarily, but the older men looked askance at the matter. Indeed, repeated and strongly emphasized Orders, and even forcible measures, were often necessary in order to make up the required contingents, not to speak of the cases in which *the recruiting led to uprisings and revolts,* of which several were of a serious nature. It is to be expected that the obligatory service will not be more favourably received by the natives than the volunteer recruiting."

According to my information this is what has happened. Conscription has naturally led to much unsettlement and disaffection amongst the natives, and this cannot but have dangerous repercussions in native territories under the rule of other European Powers. French reports show that in order to avoid being conscripted for military service in time of peace many thousands of natives are emigrating to the British colonies.[4] That, on the other hand, the native soldiers who have seen service in Europe exercise a bad influence upon their fellow-natives on their return to their homelands is a conclusion accepted by all with expert knowledge of African conditions. Complaints of this nature from French officials in Africa are already on record.[5]

It is to the credit of Great Britain that her colonies are free from the French system of militarizing the natives, though the Amritsar trial held in London in May and June of last year showed that some at least of the recruiting of her Indian soldiers for the war in Europe closely followed the old press-gang methods.[6]

II. Who Let Loose the Dogs of War in the Colonies?

But there is more to be said in reply to the baseless charge against Germany of the militarization of her colonies and native populations. It is a plain and incontrovertible fact that we were neither prepared for the war in the colonies nor did we engineer it. All responsible men in Germany as well as in the colonies, whether in public or private positions, had no doubt about the fact that the provocation of wars in Africa, in which black men under European leadership would be forced to fight against white men, would deal a deadly blow to the prestige of the white race among the blacks, and this has actually occurred. They were also of the opinion that the extension of conflicts between European nations to the African peoples was contrary to that spirit of humanity which should inspire modern colonization, a spirit which had also found expression in the Congo Act of February 26, 1885. This also determined the attitude of the German Secretary for the Colonies, who attempted, though in vain, to preserve the neutrality of at least those territories that came under the Congo Act. The German Governors were also anxious to prevent the extension of the war to the colonies, if only the attitude of the enemy had given them the least possibility of effecting this.

Owing to vindictive propaganda the impression has been created that Germany had herself carried the war into the colonies. This is untrue. In all the German colonies hostilities were begun, not by the Germans, but by their enemies. But a question of far greater importance than that of the first opening of hostilities along the frontiers is the question, *Who first made it possible that war should be waged in the German colonies at all, especially in those districts which should and would have been preserved from war by virtue of the Congo Act, if the interests of the native populations had influenced the Allied Powers at all?* The free-trade zone described in this Act included the German colonies of German East Africa and a part of the Cameroons, the British colonies of British East Africa, bordering on German East Africa, Uganda, Nyasaland, a part of Northern Rhodesia, and of the French colonies about one-half of French Equatorial Africa, bordering on the Cameroons.

In Article II of the Congo Act the signatories, who included not only Germany but Great Britain, France, and Belgium, had pledged themselves in the event of war to do their utmost to bring about the neutralization of all the territories belonging to the Congo Basin. The treaty proceeded to declare:

> *"The belligerent parties would be required from this time to refrain from carrying on hostilities in the neutralised territories and from using them as a base for warlike operations."*

It was in accordance with this clear and unmistakable treaty obligation that the Belgian Government, through its diplomatic representative at Paris, broached the subject with the French Government on August 8, 1914, expressing its desire that the Congo Basin should be neutralized, as was intended and indeed guaranteed.[7] The French Foreign Minister reported on August 9th that his Government was disposed to declare the neutrality of the Congo Basin and had requested Spain to propose this to the German Government. But soon other influences began to make themselves felt in Paris. On August 16th the Belgian Minister there reported that the French representative had told him that Spain had not yet returned an answer, since she was not acquainted with the views of the British Government. It appeared that England was still maintaining silence on the subject. The French representative had furthermore expressed the opinion that

> "it was in accordance with the present situation that Germany should be struck wherever it was possible to reach her. He was also of the opinion that this was England's point of view, and

that England would make certain definite claims: France wanted to recover that part of the Congo which she had been forced to cede as a result of the Agadir incident."

On August 17th the Belgian Minister in London reported that *the British Government declined to accept the Belgian proposal,* and that German troops in German East Africa had already undertaken an offensive against the British Protectorate of Central Africa, while, on the other hand, British troops had already attacked the harbour of Dar-es-Salam, where they had destroyed the wireless station. Under these circumstances the British Government would not be able to accept the Belgian proposal, even if it were convinced of its political and strategic expediency. The British Government also believed that the forces it was despatching to Africa would suffice to crush all resistance.

In order to put this British declaration in its proper light it is necessary to make it clear that the British attack upon Dar-es-Salam took place on August 8, 1914, and that another attack upon the inner southwestern boundary of German East Africa and the seizure of a German steamer followed on August 13th. *The first German counter-attack was made on August 15th, at Taveta.*

On August 23rd the German Government applied to the American Government and requested it to bring about an agreement with the other belligerents which would keep the **Congo Basin** immune from war. The French, taking a leaf out of the book of their British Allies, now refused upon the alleged ground that the Germans had first opened up hostilities against the French possessions. This statement was equally baseless. The first hostile act in these African districts was perpetrated by the French in their sudden attack on August 6, 1914, upon the German frontier posts of Bonga and Singa, which were as yet totally ignorant that war had broken out. The Belgians, too, by their seizure of a German official engaged upon a peaceful mission to the Belgian Congo on August 6, 1914, a date on which German East Africa was without any knowledge of Belgium's participation in hostilities, committed the first act of war. They also confiscated the official's dhau or conveyance. Only thereafter did German troops attack Belgian posts (viz. on August 15th), though this was not known to the Belgian Government for some time after its endeavour to win its Allies for neutralization had failed.

It must be obvious to every open-minded critic that the Entente Powers regarded the German colonies, cut off as they were from every communication with home, as an easy spoil of war, which they had no intention of forgoing. The idea of neutralization, which arose in Belgium and was echoed at first in France, but never once found favour in England, was soon swept aside. The Allies simply threw the Congo Act overboard as inconvenient and an obstacle to their designs. It followed that they were able with their navies to cut off the German Protectorates by sea, and to direct vastly superior forces against these isolated colonies, which in a military sense lay weak and unprotected - an easy prey. Whatever resistance was possible was offered, and acts of great heroism were done; but, entirely unprepared as they were, and incapable of prolonged defence against European armies, favoured with unlimited possibilities of pushing up reserves, they were bound in the end to be overcome, as they were. To declare in these circumstances that the colonial war was begun by the Germans is simply to say that black is white.

Exactly the same condition of things is found to exist when we examine the case of the colonies lying outside the basin of the Congo, and therefore unaffected by the restrictions of the international Congo Act. The chief administrative official of the German colony of **Togo** made the proposal to the governor of the neighbouring British colony to introduce the neutralization of the African territories. His proposal was rejected. The British and French, with their superior forces, soon broke the resistance of the small Protectorate police force and took possession of this German territory.

The first act of war in **German South-West Africa** was the surprise attack of a British force on the German frontier station Raman's Drift on September 14, 1914. Only two days later, on September 16th, did German troops attack the British settlement of Nakab.

No German attacks at all were possible in the **South Sea Islands,** for there were no ships and no military. New Guinea was fallen upon and captured by the Australians in a military expedition, Samoa by the New Zealanders, while the South Sea Islands north of the Equator were seized by Japan.

With regard to the two largest German colonies, **German East Africa** and **German South-West Africa,** there are proofs that Great Britain had made plans for capturing these in the event of an Anglo-German war. These preparations were made years before the outbreak of the World War. The leading Dutch newspaper in South Africa, *Die Burger,* made revelations with regard to these colonial war preparations in a leading article in its issue of February 22, 1923. According to these the question was discussed at the Imperial Conference in London in 1907, and a collaboration of the Home and Dominion General Staffs was resolved upon. At the Imperial Conference of 1911, the attention of the representatives of the Dominions was called to the dangerous state of affairs in Europe, and the British Committee for the Defence of the Empire invited them to draw up a plan of campaign in which they were to make clear the steps, of a military or civil nature, which they would propose to take in the event of the outbreak of war in Europe. The Government of the South African Union, the head of which at that time was General Botha, drew up such a plan in agreement with the wishes of the British Committee named and the British General Staff. This contemplated an attack on German South-West Africa and the seizure of German East Africa in the eventuality envisaged. Thus General Botha's Government in 1914-1916 merely carried out designs which had been prepared three years before.

The seizure of these two German colonies was also prepared for in detail. Propagandism directed against German South-West Africa, containing exaggerated reports of the strength and number of the German Protectorate troops, and falsely alleging the intention to attack the South African Union, was common in British South Africa before the war. The Union Defence Act of 1912, which made the Union troops liable for service anywhere in South Africa, even outside the Union, had German South-West Africa specially in view, as was stated in the Union Parliament. Indeed, the only other colonial Power in South Africa besides Germany was and is Portugal, who is united to Great Britain both by an ancient alliance and by close interest. Numbers of British subjects, in the guise of prospectors, commercial travellers, traders, etc., carried on systematic investigations and espionage in South-West Africa, and many of them returned to the colony with General Botha as British officers after the outbreak of the war. The maps used by the South African expeditionary troops during the campaign were more exact as to the waterways, wells, pastures, and other matters of military importance than those used by the Germans themselves, as was discovered by the German troops who occasionally captured the owners of such maps.[8]

The British Consul in Lüderitz Bay during journeys in the South-West before the war took exact observations of the country, particularly the south and the south-eastern frontier, where the invading troops later marched in. These journeys lasted for months. This same Consul reappeared at Lüderitz Bay at the beginning of the war as the commander of a section of troops, and brought with him everything necessary, even to a condenser for supplying the place with water - equipment which could only have been available if prepared for long beforehand. There are other proofs, besides those mentioned, that the British military authorities had for years anticipated war against German South-West Africa, and had provided for the eventuality.

The same thing occurred in German East Africa. A year and a half before the outbreak of war a British Consul there had spied out the land with great thoroughness; this, indeed, seemed to be his principal occupation. The result of his observations is plainly revealed in the *Field Notes on German East Africa. General Staff, India* (printed in Simla) which was used as a source of information by the British troops during the campaign.[9]

No less a witness than General Botha himself can be cited as proving the existence before the war of British designs - however far they may have been elaborated - against Germany's oversea dominions. In 1909, General Botha, later Prime Minister of the South African Union, who was staying at Kissingen, advised the German Pastor Schowalter, with whom he was on intimate terms, that he should seek an opportunity to warn the Berlin Government in confidence that they would not be able to avoid a war with England. Botha told him that he had become convinced of this in the course of the Imperial Conference, adding that whatever Germany might do, the war would prove unavoidable. Botha told him that this warning was meant to serve as a thank-offering for the good-will and help rendered to the Boers by the German people. Pastor Schowalter endeavoured in vain, through the agency of the Bavarian ambassador, to obtain an audience with the German Imperial Chancellor, Prince Bülow, in order to impart to him this important information. At last, shortly before the outbreak of the war, he published Botha's words of warning.[10]

A year before the outbreak of the World War, that is, in 1913, another Boer of high standing sent a similar indirect warning to the German Government to the effect that at British instigation the South African Union would be prepared to attack South-West Africa, and was making preparations to that end. I have this information from a thoroughly reliable source.

Government hospital, Dar-es-Salam, German East Africa

Hospital for natives suffering from sleeping sickness at Udjidji, German East Africa

Queen Charlotte Hospital, Lome, Togoland

Railway bridge (span 159.60 metres), Sanaga South Branch, The Cameroons

Cable railway in Usambara, German East Africa

6

The Allied Powers and Their "Sacred Trust"

The policy followed by Germany in her Protectorates was of an altogether different character from that represented in the diplomatic Notes, Handbooks, and other propaganda of her enemies, and in certain important particulars, as will be shown, it compares more than favourably with that of the Allied Powers. The real goal of that policy has been repeatedly made clear by the responsible German authorities and spokesmen in this field, both in speeches in the Reichstag and in print. Dr. Dernburg, one of the later Secretaries of State for the Colonies, emphatically declaring that "the native was the most valuable asset of our colonies," continually urged that all the efforts of German colonization must be directed first towards providing for and preserving him. Among his successors, Dr. von Lindequist also made it clear that benevolent treatment of the native population was a sine qua non of German colonial policy. Dr. Solf, who was Secretary for the Colonies before and during the World War, plainly promulgated his ideals in Reichstag speeches and in books in the expressive phrase: "Colonizing means missionizing." "An active colonial policy," he said long before the war, "does not mean only the exploitation of such countries according to the measure of the home country's needs, but also co-operation in a great task which cultured humanity is obliged to fulfil towards the tribes of these territories - the task of training them morally and intellectually, and of creating the conditions for their economic development as well as being helpful to them in obtaining a higher degree of human development."

Again, in a speech made in the Reichstag as late as March 6, 1913, he described Germany's attitude towards the natives as follows:

> "The natives are our *protégés* and the German Government must for their sakes assume the obligation of making the interests of the natives its own. For we do not wish to exterminate the natives, but to preserve them. That is the moral duty which we assumed when we hoisted the German flag in our colonies and in the South Seas. The performance of this duty is also in accordance with wisdom. For this alone gives us the possibility of a rational economic policy, and thereby the basis for our participation in the same."

All the foregoing sentiments and many others like them in humane tendency were uttered and acted on before the war broke the continuity of administration in the German colonies, and that is why Dr. Solf was able with a good conscience to nail to the counter the many misstatements which were circulated as part of a nefarious war propaganda with a view to discrediting his country in the eyes of the world and paving the way for the annexation of these territories if the fortunes of war went against it. Defending German colonial policy in 1915 against the calumnies which had already begun, he wrote:

> "In all the colonies in Africa and in the South Seas, the German Government has established other and more liberal principles in the field of administration as well as in commercial life, in the matter of military occupation, in trade and transportation, in the railway system, in agriculture, etc., than was possible in the mother country. Not a single colony of ours is

subject to a military administration. If militarism were the ideal of the Germans, if the Germans had the warlike qualities and the ambitions of the *conquistadores,* which have been attributed to them, then our colonies would furnish a natural proof of this, for they would have been a welcome breeding-ground for the alleged militarism and wanton soldiery. It is more than remarkable that this is not so, that we have introduced a peaceful civilian *régime,* and that we have not transplanted those institutions and restrictions, which have become a historic necessity in Germany for protecting our frontiers, to those new countries which we now govern and in which we have allowed everything to develop in a spirit of freedom."[1]

If I may be permitted to add my own verdict to the voices of those other men who were appointed to govern the colonies, then as the last Governor of German East Africa, the largest of Germany's colonies, I would say that both before and during the war it was always my policy, as it was that of my predecessors, to make the welfare of the natives entrusted to my care the dominant feature of my administration. This was manifested not only in protecting the natives against all oppression by whites or blacks, and in giving them the benefit of social welfare laws relating to employment, but also in extensive sanitary measures, in campaigns against epidemics, and in a system of scientific hygiene. The same thing applied to the mental and moral improvement of the blacks by means of good schools and by inducing them to improve their agricultural methods. I doubt whether any English or French colony with the same natural conditions and the same kind of population could boast of excelling or even equalling us in this field. The same system prevailed in the other German colonies, and in most of them great things were achieved precisely in the spheres of hygiene and of education.

An objective description of German colonial policy will be found in the *Deutsches Koloniallexikon,* a work which could not appear until after the end of the war, but which was already complete for publication at the outbreak of the war, and was published afterwards without alterations. In that work the late Professor Rathgen, a distinguished expert, famous alike for his scientific eminence and his absolute objectivity, writes as follows with regard to the German policy of treating the natives:

> "Not only is the native in need of guardianship, but he must be especially protected against exploitation, usury, and proletarization, just as much as against disease and famine. It is, of course, in its own interest that a far-seeing colonial policy should treat the natives with care and consideration. The necessity of there being some higher authority, standing above the possible conflict of interests between the white and the native population, is the principal argument against the granting of absolute autonomy to the white population of colonies with a mixed population."[2]

Are not these principles, proclaimed by the most influential colonial politicians of Germany, leading statesmen, as well as representatives of the sciences, such as might be set up by any progressive modern nation? Is there anything in them which the authors of the libellous pamphlets on Germany's colonial record could regard as an excuse for their language? Do they promulgate or countenance purposes and aims which are not in perfect agreement with those laid down in the articles of the League of Nations?

And now let us consider how the Allied Powers, after proclaiming to the world their recognition of responsibility for the welfare of the natives as a "sacred trust of civilization," have fulfilled that trust in the case of Germany's colonies. In callous disregard of every consideration of humanity, and in violation of the very principles of the League of Nations, France has been given *carte blanche* to carry on her militarizing policy in the native territories entrusted to her by Mandate! Do all British and American friends of the League of Nations know this, and understand what it means? The story of this pitiful episode must be briefly told. How Germany would have been accused of barbarity and fiendishness had she been guilty of such conduct!

According to the rules of the League of Nations all militarization of the German colonies should be prohibited in the interests of the native population. How, in spite of this fact, France succeeded in securing a clause in her Mandates over the Cameroons and Togoland entitling her to employ the black inhabitants of these territories for her military ends, even in Europe, is one of the blackest chapters in the history of the Versailles Treaty. This betrayal of great native populations, which have been handed over body and soul to French militarism, has also unquestionably shaken the faith of thousands in the League of Nations, and has struck a fatal blow at the enthusiasm of even the credulous idealists of Germany, who had really believed in the pure motives of the League, and were prepared to regard it as indicating a move forward in the march of humanity and of public morality.

Mr. Baker's book on Wilson, from which quotations have already been made, throws light on the incident. According to his explicit account, Pichon, the French representative on the Council of Ten, demanded on January 10, 1919, the right to conscript colonial troops in the territories to be placed under French Mandate. Lloyd George replied,

> "What is forbidden by the documents would be a mode of procedure such as the Germans would probably employ, that is to organize great black armies in Africa, in order to drive everyone else out of the country.[3] There is nothing in these documents which would prevent France from conscripting an army for the defence of her territory" (i.e. the mandated territory).

Clemenceau declared that he would be satisfied if France had the right, in the event of a great war, to conscript troops in the African territories under her rule. Lloyd George said that as long as Clemenceau did not recruit large negro armies for purposes of aggression, this was all that the clause was intended to prevent! Clemenceau, of course, replied that the latter was not his intention. He would, therefore, assume that Lloyd George's interpretation was correct, and he declared himself perfectly satisfied.[4] Nevertheless, in the Committee for the League of Nations, the French again attempted to force through their original demands, but the wording proposed by General Smuts was accepted and became part of the statutes of the League.

Three days before the Peace Treaty was handed to the Germans, when everything was in great confusion and all hands busily occupied in completing the document, Clemenceau arbitrarily and *without consulting his colleagues of the Big Four, or the members of the Committee for the League of Nations,* who had charge of the statutes of the League, gave orders to the copyists through their colleague, M. Fromageot, to alter the wording of the statute of the League of Nations in such a way that the Mandatories of the colonies should be expressly permitted to recruit troops, not only in order to uphold order in the colonies, but also, if need be, for use in defence of the mother country.[5]

On May 5th renewed discussions took place on this point between Wilson, Clemenceau, and Lloyd George. Sir Maurice Hankey, Secretary of the Copying Bureau, read the following report: "The alteration in Article 22 (Statutes of the League of Nations, treating of colonies and mandates) was made *under instructions given personally to M. Fromageot by M. Clemenceau,* the President of the Conference." Upon this Clemenceau declared it to be of the utmost importance for France that a few words should be inserted "to enable France to use coloured troops for the defence of French territory, just as in the present war." President Wilson called attention to the discussion which had taken place on January 30th in the Council of Ten, when it was agreed that precisely the same wording in the Resolution on the Mandates, namely, prohibition of the military training of the natives "for other than for police purposes and for the defence of territories," would suffice France's needs.[6]

It was determined not to use the unauthorized French wording, but to restore the clause in its original form, as in the statutes of the League of Nations. Even now the French did not give way, but transferred their operations to the Commission appointed to work out the rules for the Mandates and to the League of Nations. Accordingly when the plan for the French Mandate over the Cameroons and Togoland was laid before the Council of the League on December 20, 1920, the following condition was inserted in Article 3: "It is understood, however, that the troops so raised (in the French Cameroons and Togoland) may, in the event of a general war, be utilized to repulse an attack or for defence of territory outside that over which the Mandate is administered."

When this condition was made known to the Secretariat of the League of Nations in Geneva, the commentary on the official report contained these words: "The Secretariat quotes the clause appertaining to Article 22 of the Treaty of the League, which appears to be in contradiction to the foregoing permission."

In point of fact, the French Mandates - and only these - were fitted with this additional clause and so came into operation. Thus the intentions of the explicit principles of the League of Nations were vitiated by being converted *into their exact opposite.* The French are authorized to militarize the native population of their mandated territory, the Cameroons and Togoland, precisely in the same manner as the inhabitants of their own colonies, *and this they have lost no time in doing.* For already they have introduced the French military laws of Equatorial Africa and West Africa, prescribing the conscription of native soldiers and compulsory service in foreign countries into the mandated territories, the Cameroons, and Togoland.[7] In the Report of the Army Commission of March 18, 1924, to the French Chamber of Deputies it is stated (page 809) that " the future international situation of this possession (the Cameroons) should enable us to make it participate in the military efforts which we expect from our African Empire." *("La situation internationale future doit nous permettre de la faire participer à l'effort militaire que nous réclamons de notre empire africain.")*[8]

How the recruiting is carried out is described in the same Report in the words: "The manner of recruiting was not free from grave mistake, and the methods practised provoked troubles of the first order, which led to rebellions in some quarters." Light was thrown upon these vile methods in December, 1924, when the law suit of Diagne (native member of the French Chamber of Deputies for Senegal) against the chief editor of the journal *Les Continents* was being heard. In this process it was proved that a French Governor needed a whole arsenal to enforce "voluntary recruiting." His requisitions included 15,000 hand grenades, 30,000 various gas grenades, four aeroplanes, and numerous white troops! Such methods are henceforth to be used against the poor natives of the former settled and prosperous German colonies of the Cameroons and Togoland with the authority of the League of Nations, *and the passive assent, to say the least, of Great Britain and America.*

Henceforth, until the conscience of the world awakens in righteous indignation, France will be able to employ the natives of the German colonies, so long as they remain under her rule, as of her other colonies, in warfare of any kind, aggressive or defensive, in any part of the globe, including the European Continent. That is the point of the boast of General Mangin, the author of the scheme of a great French black army, and repeated by ex-President Poincaré, that "France is a nation no longer of forty, but of one hundred millions," the male section of which is liable to military service anywhere and everywhere. The drafting of late German native subjects into the French army has already begun. A private letter on the conditions prevailing in the Cameroons since the French occupation states that a number of natives who were recruited as soldiers by the French in 1919 and 1920 have returned wounded to that territory, reporting that they fought in Morocco and that many others are believed to have fallen there.

Such proceedings turn the whole Mandate project into a horrible mockery. They are in crassest contradiction to all that the League of Nations claims to stand for, above all to that "sacred trust of civilization," to the fulfilment of which the mandatory Powers solemnly pledged themselves.

This militarization of the blacks, however, is also a crime against both races, the white and the black. The training in course of time of hundreds of thousands of blacks in European methods of warfare and the use of modern weapons, putting them in positions of authority over whites of a vastly higher stage of culture, such as was done in wartime in West Africa with German prisoners of war, cannot but involve the gravest danger to the future of the white race. But this is not the worst. The blacks were actually given such positions of authority *on European soil,* on the Rhine and in the Ruhr district. German women were violated by blacks in these regions, and German local administrative authorities were forced to institute brothels with white women for the use of the black troops! All these unspeakable outrages upon the white race, which will never be forgotten or forgiven by Germans, were instituted by the French; and, disregarding considerations of morality, which nowadays do not count as they once did, a more short-sighted piece of criminal folly could not well be imagined. The prestige of the white race, upon which, for the greater part, the white man's rule in Africa depends, has thus been permanently undermined, and to-day it is in the direst peril. Even the native population of the colonies under the ban of French militarism is subjected to grave dangers. Many black soldiers shipped to Europe fall victims to the unaccustomed climate, while others, as a Frenchman himself has written, "lose their native virtues and bring home new vices, such as drunkenness. They lose their mental and moral balance, since they have outgrown their natural sphere of action; they become shy of work, and form an element that succumbs easily to political agitation and becomes the cause of riot and rebellion." "One day or other," adds this writer, "the older natives, discontented, and the young ones, torn up by the roots, will unite against us, and we shall pay dearly for our imprudence. The reports of the British authorities are unanimous in declaring that the sending to Europe of Hindoo troops was one of the initial causes of the movement which at the present time imperils British domination in India."[9]

7

The Treatment of the Natives

The Notes accompanying the Treaty of Versailles contain grave accusations against the Germans with respect to the treatment of natives in the German colonies. The proofs advanced are the statements and allegations of German official and private individuals made before the war - many long before it - and the evidence of such German party men as ex-Deputies Erzberger and Noske. The material thus collected was first given to the world in three publications - as regards German South-West Africa, in the Blue Book submitted to the House of Commons in 1918; in regard to the other colonies, the British Foreign Office Handbook on *The Treatment of Natives in German Colonies,* which has already been mentioned, and the notorious and libellous pamphlet of Evans Lewin. Apropos of the Blue Book, the reader may be referred to the *Star* of Johannesburg of November 10, 1924, according to which General Hertzog, the Prime Minister of the Union of South Africa, uttered the following words at Gobabis in the course of a journey through the mandated territory: "As to the historical Blue Book, he (General Hertzog) doubted whether anyone believed its contents. It was considered a war pamphlet - one among many that had gone into oblivion or soon would do so."

It is no pleasant task to rake up these old and long-forgotten "colonial scandals," as they were called at the time. I do not see, however, how this can be avoided. The charges based on them were repeated and used by our opponents during the war in an utterly one-sided and unscrupulous fashion. Many known truths were suppressed and many published refutations of groundless accusations were ignored, in order to prepare a "moral" pretext on which to excuse the seizure of our colonies. I feel myself competent to write of these things, since at the time of the "colonial scandals" I was Head of Staff in the Imperial Colonial Office. In that capacity I was personally engaged in following up and investigating the charges made: I studied all the ensuing documents; and I was also the author of the memorial which, at the close of the investigations, was laid before the Reichstag.

The name "colonial scandals" applies to a number of accusations brought against individual officials and officers, which in part referred to topical events, but in part went back to the very beginnings of German colonization. A large number of these cases had already made their way through the courts or been carried to a conclusion by the administrative authorities. Other cases related to investigations only just begun or never brought to a close, and in others the charges were new and the investigations in the initial stages.

These "colonial scandals" caused a great deal of excitement and high feeling in Germany. After Dr. Bernhard Dernburg, the Secretary of State, had been called upon to assume charge of the colonial administration in 1906, a commission was appointed to investigate and clear up these matters in the most thorough fashion. This commission was composed of three experienced Prussian judges, two of whom belonged to the Superior Court *(Kammergericht),* the highest Prussian court of law, and one to a Prussian *Landgericht,* also a higher court. These were all officials of absolutely unimpeachable integrity, and moreover they stood in no official relation whatever to the Government or to the colonial administration. The three officials, in an investigation which lasted for several months, studied the entire question of the "colonial scandals" in perfect quiet and immunity from all outside influences. Secretary of State Dr. Dernburg, who at that time held the post of Acting-Colonial

Director, had given orders that all documents in the possession of the Colonial Office, including those which for any reason whatever were marked in the archives as "Private," should be open to their inspection. I personally superintended their researches and saw to it that everything was made really and not merely formally accessible, and that nothing was kept secret from them. I am also an actual witness as to the exactitude and thoroughness with which this commission of judges went about its work, sparing no pains or labour to get at the real truth.[1]

I append a declaration which this judicial Commission issued in respect to its activities:

"In answer to various attacks in the Press, the Investigation Committee appointed by the Minister of Justice at the request of the Colonial Department of the Foreign Office issues the following official statement:

> "**1.** Before their investigations had begun, the Acting-Colonial Director, His Excellency Bernhard Dernburg, especially empowered the members of the Commission to demand any or all of the documents of the Colonial Office, even the most secret sealed documents, without exception, for the purpose of inspection.
>
> "**2.** The investigation proceeded along these lines. All documents demanded were at once unreservedly handed out to the members of the Commission, and no restrictions were placed upon their use.
>
> "**3.** With regard to the extent or the tendency of the investigations, no restrictions of any kind were placed upon the work of the Commission.
>
> "**4.** On the contrary, in arranging its work the Commission set up the principle that the extent of the investigation and the verdicts deduced from all evidence discovered should be determined only by the individual conviction of the members as judges. Every individual case has been judged according to these principles and

the judgment reached by the judges were made according to their free and independent judgment, without any attempt whatsoever being made to influence them from any direction.

"Berlin, April 12, 1907.

"(Signed)

"DR. KLEINE, Councillor of the Superior Court.

"OELSCHLAEGER, Councillor of the Superior Court.

"WILKE, Councillor of the Superior County Court."

This Commission, after the most exhaustive examination, and when necessary after supplementing the material in hand, delivered its verdict upon each individual case. The result of this judicial examination was then laid before the Reichstag in the form of a Report (Reichstag Print No. 288) on April 15, 1907. When this Report was discussed in the Budget Commission of the Reichstag, the entire mass of documents from the Colonial Office pertaining to it was at disposal, and the Secretary of State for the Colonies declared himself ready to furnish in person or through the mouth of his commissioner any further information desired by members of the Reichstag, so that there was no suggestion of any attempt at concealment. The Reichstag did not discuss the matter further, however, thereby signifying its opinion that these judicial reports were to be regarded as the final settlement of the scandals.

All these proceedings are utterly ignored in the Handbooks which were supplied as reliable and comprehensive sources of information to the Peace Conference Delegations in Paris, and also in all the various propagandist pamphlets and speeches levelled at the time against German colonial administration. In these publications and utterances the "colonial scandals" are represented *in the light in which they appeared when the first charges were brought by members of the Reichstag and before any investigation had taken place.* The charges are put forward as if they were proven and accepted facts, and the officials concerned as convicted criminals, guilty of established cruelties. This was by no means the case. Yet the suppressed verdict of the judicial Commission in a great number of cases was to the effect that "investigations have brought nothing incriminating to light," or "no cause can be established for proceeding against the accused in a disciplinary or punitive sense."

Many of the officials who had been unjustly accused were acquitted not only in a judicial but also in a moral sense, and occupied posts of honour for many years afterwards. In a number of other cases the Commission established the fact that the defendants had been guilty of breaches of the law, though in nearly all these cases penalties had *already been imposed* either through the courts or the administration. In so far as acts of great brutality or cruelty had occurred, it was proved that these had been committed in almost every case by men not quite normal - those who had suffered from nervous shocks or strains incidental to tropical conditions of life, and the like - yet these cases none the less aroused the greatest indignation and repugnance among all classes of Germans.

As an illustration of the manner in which truth has been disregarded in making use of all possible accusations of ill-treatment of the natives, it should suffice to inform the reader that both in the Lewin pamphlet and in the official Handbook named, *stories which had long before been proved to be mere inventions were again circulated as if they were true* - surely, a method of controversy abhorrent to honourable men. One of the worst examples is that of the ogreish legend of the drowning of fifty small children in the Nachtigal Falls by one Captain Dominik. The author of this story, a West African trader, from whom the late August Bebel, who narrated it in the Reichstag, received his information direct, was brought to book in 1909, and declared before the judge that *his charges were without any foundation in fact.* All the leading German newspapers at the time printed long and detailed reports of the case and the evidence, and it is morally certain that the facts were made known by the British Press. Yet the calumny was resuscitated.

Let it be admitted that the past history of the German colonies was not free from cases of ill-treatment of natives and even acts of cruelty. Yet it is sheer pharisaism for other nations to cast stones upon the

German people because of such occurrences. The colonial history of *no* nation is free from excesses, and indeed it would be easy to prove cases elsewhere exceeding in gravity anything to be found in the short history of German colonization. Even to-day analogous instances are constantly occurring.

Anyone with a fondness for the work would be able to draw up long and heavy indictments against the French, Belgian, Portuguese, and British colonial *régimes* by the use of authenticated material contained in parliamentary papers and speeches, reports of law-court proceedings, and the like. Take only several quite recent analogies by way of example and also of warning.

The brutal treatment of the Moroccans by the French during the years immediately preceding the war is related in a striking little book entitled *Light for John Bull on the Moroccan Question,* by Charles Rosher (London, 1911). (See particularly the chapter on "Pacific Penetration.") Take, again, the cruelties in the French colonies which were reported by Deputy Boisneuf during the session of the French Chamber of Deputies on November 10, 1921.[2] It is certain that nothing worse than these occurs in the history of any German colony. It is also a matter of common knowledge how the late Mr. E. D. Morel revealed in all its horrifying detail the terrible martyrdom of the natives in the Belgian and French Congo.[3] In his book *Present Conditions in the Congo* (1911) the Rev. John H. Harris, organizing secretary of the English Anti-Slavery Society, summarizes the condition of things in the Belgian Congo under King Leopold as follows:

> "In most districts something was given to the natives, but it was of infinitesimal value, frequently being limited to a few spoonfuls of salt. This, however, was never regarded as payment, but merely a gratuity at the discretion of the white official, M. de Smet de Naeyer having publicly declared with brutal frankness, 'The native is entitled to nothing; what is given to him is a

mere gratuity.' The medium used for extorting this flow of virgin produce ('rubber, ivory and gum opal') was force, which in the Congo expressed itself in hostage-taking, pillage, and murder."

Morel's protests against the brutal methods which were actually exterminating the natives of the Congo regions were crowned with success; the Belgians and French were compelled to revise their methods. Such methods of procedure, amounting to ruthless, unintelligent exploitation, cannot be given the name of colonization. It is needless to say that nothing of that kind can be laid to Germany's account, nor, to be just, to that of Great Britain.

Nevertheless, according to Mr. Harris, just quoted, the condition of the Congo just before the war still left much to be desired. His book, *Present Conditions in the Congo*, consists of reports on his investigations in that region in 1911, and therein he states that while a great improvement had taken place in certain directions "much of the old *régime* remains, and what is of graver moment, the greater part of the *personnel* appears to be wedded to the corrupting principles of Leopoldianism." Taxation was excessive; he found a system of "justice" to exist which required aggrieved suitors to "tramp a distance equivalent to a return journey between London and Newcastle and even then keeps them waiting outside the court for over two years"; and forced labour prevailed on the rubber plantations. He writes:

> "A native chief expressed the opinion that the Belgian Government is going the same way as the old Congo State. 'First a little rubber in the hand; then baskets of it - failing which, the whip and the prison-house'" (p. 13 of report of December 6, 1911).

The significant remark occurs: "The very word 'rubber' is sufficient to strike terror into the mind of the average native."

Comparing Belgian with German colonies, Harris writes:

"In comparing the position of natives in German Togoland with that of the Congo natives, it must be borne in mind that the former are generally speaking fairly well off, and receive large benefits from the German occupation, whereas to-day the greater part of the Congo territory is in a worse condition than when Stanley crossed it in 1877, and the natives themselves are completely impoverished " (p. 12 of report of August 23, 1911).

Harris writes in his *Dawn in Darkest Africa:* " Belgium finds herself in possession of a colonial colony... whose native tribes everywhere mistrust her administration." So her Allies, in the discharge of their "sacred trust," have given her more African territory and more native tribes to govern!

This writer has also much to say of Portuguese maladministration in colonial regions. Referring, in the same book, to the West African possessions of Portugal, he records the "widespread plantation slavery in Angola, San Thomé, and Principe," endorses the estimate that half the population of Angola was then "living under some form of slavery," though the admonitions of the British Foreign Office had led to an improvement, and speaks of the system of flogging still prevalent. He writes:

"The island of Principe has a horror all its own, for it is infested with the dread sleeping sickness.... The slaves of Principe present an even more melancholy appearance than do those of San Thome. They appear to have an instinctive knowledge that they are confined in a death-trap and their appeals for liberation are piteously violent."[4]

In his introduction to Mr. Harris's book the late Lord Cromer wrote under date October, 1912:

"In spite of the long-standing friendship between the two countries, in spite of historical associations which are endeared to all Englishmen, and in spite of the apparently unequivocal nature of treaty engagements, it would, I feel assured, be quite impossible, should the African possessions of Portugal be seriously menaced, for British arms to be employed in order to retain them under the uncontrolled possession of Portugal so long as slavery is permitted."

Further, in his book *Portuguese Slavery: Britain's Dilemma*, published in 1913, Harris writes:

"It is maintained that the pages of this book establish, first, the existence of slave owning and slave trading; secondly, that this is a crime committed against international law; thirdly, that it is the imperative duty of the European Powers to demand the cessation of this crime, but that it continues to flourish under the protection of Great Britain."

I am willing to hope charitably that the abuses recorded as existing in the colonies of Great Britain's ally in 1912 did not exist in 1917. But what shall be said of accusers who in that year had to go back to the beginning of the century in order to make out their "justification" for appropriating Germany's colonies, though these have been held up by English authorities as offering to the natives better conditions than Belgian, Portuguese, or even French colonies?

Both Morel and Harris have been frank and fair-minded enough to condemn regrettable episodes and excesses in British territories, as English people must know better than I. How far Mr. Morel is an acceptable authority on these or other matters in England I do not profess to know, but I would protest with every right that it is not for people who still persist in crediting the often frivolous and more often baseless charges which were brought in pre-war times by German Social

Democratic deputies and journalists against the Government of our colonial empire - which, to be sure, many of them never wanted, and would have given away to the first applicant - to pooh-pooh and reject Morel's countercharges as necessarily fictitious, and say: "We are prepared to believe anything said by a German Socialist and Labour man against Germany, but we will believe nothing whatever that an English Socialist and Labour man may say against us and our Allies." Such a method of controversy should be repugnant to every decent mind, and moreover its very employment is a confession that the case defended is weak and not very creditable.

To go, however, to other witnesses, during the session of the British House of Commons of July 4, 1923, Mr. Snell, M.P., brought a charge to the effect that in Kenya, British East Africa, in the course of the last few years natives had either been whipped to death by whites or had died in consequence of ill-treatment. One case occurred in 1920, the delinquent being only convicted by a white jury of "simple hurt," and a still worse in June, 1923, the white murderer in this instance, when likewise tried by a white jury, being sent to prison for two years. This native was flogged by a white settler until he was tired, and then by two black employees in turn until their victim collapsed. A detailed account of this shocking case (with two others), written by Mr. Harris, with the title "Flogging in Kenya," appeared in the *Manchester Guardian* of November 16, 1923. Dr. Norman Keys also deals with this case, and the subject of white cruelty to natives generally, in his book *Kenya*, published in 1924, adding:

> "Such floggings are neither rebuked by the general opinion of Kenya nor punished by the law, while men like Kitosh (the murdered native), who try to escape from brutal masters, are hunted down by the police, severely punished, and compelled to complete their contracts of service" (see pp. 159-69).

It was in relation to Kenya that the Archbishop of Canterbury, speaking in the House of Lords on May 20, 1925, admitted that there had been "scandalous cases" of ill-treatment, though he protested justifiably against generalizations. Lord Buckmaster, who followed him, was not so lenient, for he stated:

> "Certain events which had happened in Kenya recently had undoubtedly shocked everyone who had been made acquainted with the facts. He agreed entirely that it would be a serious injustice that all these acts - some of which were acts of unredeemed brutality - should be regarded as symptomatic of the general conduct of the settlers in that country. They obviously were not. He knew that such cases might not infrequently occur where white people in tropical countries dealt with the native population. But the thing that had seriously affected his mind was the fact that when the people who committed these acts were brought before the court they were not justly and adequately punished. It did not appear that their conduct was publicly reprobated. The natives at present had no security in the reserves that they occupied. They had no guarantee that further parts of their land might not from time to time, as it was thought fit, be taken away and allotted to other settlers.... He was most anxious to see that the natives were not allowed to be used for the creation of wealth which they did not share. In the past there had been a policy of attempting to put pressure on the natives to induce them to leave their reserves and to work for the white man. He wanted an assurance from the Government that that pressure was going to cease. Things had been happening in Kenya which could never have happened in India and had never happened in any other part of the Empire. He wanted to be assured that those things would not happen again and that we should do everything to discharge to the native population the solemn duties which we had undertaken on their behalf."

Lord Balfour wound up the discussion in a speech in which he uttered the ambiguous words: "Without dogmatizing, *we must assume* that one mission which we had deliberately undertaken was that of benefiting the natives by civilizing the country in which they lived and by making them sharers in that civilization." It is only necessary to add that while the indictment made against German colonial administration in part goes back thirty years, the condition of things revealed by Lord Buckmaster as existing in a British colony *refers to the present time.*[5]

Let us be honest, however, and admit that such episodes will always occur so long as "man's inhumanity to man" is a factor to be reckoned with. The record of every colonizing country is stained with dark blots, for the most benevolent colonial administration in the world cannot wholly protect all its black subjects against harshness and abuse. All that it can do is to prosecute delinquents with the utmost diligence and to see, as far as is possible, that all evil elements are eliminated. That this was done by the German Government, especially in the years preceding the war, can be disputed by no one who is conversant with the actual facts. It is a Frenchman, Alcide Ebray, who writes in *La Paix malpropre,* published in 1924:

> "Whoever has studied colonial history at all knows that every nation committed misdeeds against the natives and that no nation is entitled to accuse another in this respect. It would not be possible to prove that Germany ill-treated natives in a higher degree than the other colonizing Powers."

It is the weakest part of the indictment manufactured by our assailants that in the diplomatic Notes addressed to Germany and in the Handbook on the treatment of the natives of her protectorates the charges of oppression, cruelty, and the like are made generally, and levelled against the entire colonial administration since its earliest beginnings in 1884. Cruelty to the natives, arbitrary requisitions, punishment by whipping, insufficient protective laws, and bad treatment of the chiefs are said to have been characteristic of the administration, and to have led to grave native rebellions and sanguinary punitive expeditions.

In order to prove these charges a number of cases are cited and members of the Reichstag are named as evidence. But the greater part of these accusations lose point when the condition of the German colonies before the Germans took them over is compared with their condition immediately before the World War. Previous to 1884 the colonies were savage countries where every man's hand was against his neighbour and "war of all against all" was the rule. The native tribes were continually robbing and murdering one another. In many parts of East Africa the wandering nomads persistently made plundering inroads upon the peaceful agricultural tribes. Coming from the wild interior, these nomads would break through to the coast, destroying in their progress all the foundations and promise of an incipient civilization. On the other hand, the Arab slaving expeditions would invade the interior from the coast, creating fearful havoc. In the other German colonies in Africa similar conditions prevailed. In German New Guinea cannibalism held sway, and native hordes systematically raided one another in order to obtain human flesh. In many parts of the contiguous islands the head-hunters laid waste the coasts in their terrible and murderous expeditions.

What a different picture the German colonies presented at the outbreak of the war, after only thirty years of colonization! Peace and order reigned everywhere in the Protectorates. Robbery and murder from tribe to tribe had entirely ceased. The native went peacefully about his work. Often enough it was precisely the tribes which were formerly most warlike, most feared, and most given to robbery and plunder, which had settled most perfectly into the new order of things, and which toiled most whole-heartedly at the work of colonization.

It goes without saying that such an absolute change in the manner of life of barbarous populations could not take place without scenes of bloodshed between the native tribes which had hitherto dominated and their new rulers. The nomadic tribes which had been accustomed to increase their herds by the simple device of plundering expeditions, and the native chiefs whose existence was established upon the oppression of their subjects by sword and fire, were neither of them disposed to give up their rights without a struggle. Serious fighting was necessary before the Germans could enforce peace. But has this not been the case in every colony with a similar population? The English who had serious battles with the Zulu Kaffirs in South Africa are scarcely entitled to blame the Germans for finding it necessary to fight the relations of these very Zulu Kaffirs in East Africa in order to keep order in the country. There is enough in the annals of every colonizing Power to warn all nations of the folly and danger of throwing stones at each other and trying to pose as immaculate; for however ingenious such attempts may be, the fact remains that it is *mere posing all the time.*

Considering the atrocious charges which have been fabricated by malicious pens in order to discredit Germany and justify the seizure of her colonies, our critics must expect to hear of counter-allegations, and if fair-minded they will not allow self-pride to blind them to established facts. Nevertheless, in recalling past unhappy episodes in British colonial history, I do not do it for the purpose of making capital out of them, but only in order to suggest that equity, not to say wisdom, requires of our accusers a similar restraint.

Did not Mr. Gladstone, at the time of the Zulu War, charge the British Government of the day with responsibility for the slaying of ten thousand natives for "the only offence of attempting to defend their independence and their homes"? Is the story of all the countless Indian frontier wars so glorious that every one of them can to-day be recalled by humane Englishmen without regret or compunction? Many hard things have been written by English pens about the Matabele wars of twenty years ago; and it is not to be denied that there was a time, and it was not long ago, when the Boers of South Africa said just as hard things about the British as Germany's malicious critics say to-day about

German colonial administrators, though many of the latter have no need to fear comparison with the best of any other country.

J. H. Harris, in his book *The Chartered Millions,*[6] published only in 1920, attributes the Mashona and Matabele rising to the robbery of the natives' land and cattle, a labour system "synonymous with slavery," and an inadequately controlled police, among other causes, and says that in the hostilities the casualties (including the wounded) amongst the white settlers, police, and troops numbered 344. But he adds:

> "The losses amongst the natives were frightful: *probably the avenging of the whites has nowhere in British history assumed such terrible proportions.* Men in Rhodesia give an involuntary shudder as they recount the way in which the Mashonas who fled to the caves for protection were treated. Those who wish blood-curdling stories can easily find them in the reports of both natives and white men " (p. 130).

See also on this subject *Some Incidents in the Life of Cecil Rhodes,* by Vere Stent (Cape Town, 1925), relating Rhodes' meeting with the delegation of armed Matabele chiefs and warriors on August 21, 1896, and the terrible indictment of cruelty, cattle-thieving, and lust brought against the whites by the delegation. "It is all true," said to Rhodes one of his companions, when the recital ended.

To come to quite recent times, the action of the Mandate administration in South-West Africa in proceeding against the Bondelswarts with air-bombs, which killed many women and children among the surprised Hottentot tribe, caused a great deal of indignation throughout the world. There was the bombing of the Waziri tribesmen of an Afghan village of which the *Manchester Guardian* of June 23, 1923, wrote in a leading article headed "A Modern Atrocity." Here compensation had to be paid, since the wrong people were killed. There was also the Indian Amritsar episode which, though subsequently repudiated and condemned by the British Government, has never ceased to be defended by a large and influential section of the English people. More lately there was the bombing of the Iraq, facetiously described by the British Air Ministry as a "slight air action" in May, 1924, because a disaffected chief refused to surrender. When the last-named incident was discussed in the House of Commons a Labour member said: "That is what the Germans did to us. We called them Huns, but we are Christian soldiers."

Or, to take the case of France, since the French in the Western Soudan conquered the native chiefs by means of sanguinary battles, and are doing the same thing in Morocco to-day, can they blame the German administration in the Cameroons for the fighting which was necessary in order to secure peace in that colony? Surely no one can object to the "little wars" waged against native tribes in New Guinea, which had the amiable habit of falling upon a neighbouring tribe, making a number of prisoners, and carrying them off to be fattened for a cannibal feast? These practices could never have been put an end to by peaceful means.

With regard to revolts and punitive expeditions, an examination of the facts proves at once that the German colonies have by no means had more than their share as compared with the colonies of other nations with a similar native population. On the contrary, it is probable that the comparison is greatly in favour of the Germans. The largest colony, German East Africa, had no revolts at all since 1906 - full eight years of absolute peace in all parts of the colony. The neighbouring British colony cannot say as much, for British East Africa suffered repeatedly from revolts during this period. In 1906 occurred the revolt of the Nandi, in 1913-14 the rebellion of the Kismaji, and before this a revolt of the Massai. In British Nyasaland there was a native revolt during the late war and British Government officials were assassinated. Nothing of this kind happened either in German East Africa or in the other German colonies.

The Handbook here criticized mentions three great rebellions, which were coupled with heavy loss of life to the natives, and which are all said to have been avoidable. These were *the Arab revolt in*

German East Africa in 1888, the Maji-Maji revolt in 1905, and the Herero rebellion in German South-West Africa in 1904 - all events, be it noted, going back from twenty-one to thirty-seven years ago. The author erroneously ascribes **the Arab revolt** to arrogant behaviour on the part of the officials of the German East Africa Company, whereas it was really due to the taking over of sovereign rights on the East African coast by that Company. The Arabs, who had hitherto been masters there, saw in this step the beginning of their complete subjection, and feared that the German measures against the slave trade might destroy one of their chief sources of gain. This revolt could have been avoided only if Germany had relinquished the establishment of her authority and abandoned all measures against the seizure of slaves. The crushing of this revolt was effected by Hermann von Wissmann, a man known throughout the entire world as an honourable officer and gentleman, as well as a renowned African explorer. He proceeded with energy, but avoided all unnecessary bloodshed.

The Handbook asserts also that **the Maji-Maji revolt in Tanganyika (German East Africa)** was due to hatred of the natives, induced by the hut-tax and by forced labour upon the European plantations. The disproof of this assertion is contained in the fact that the revolt was limited to the southern part of the colony, in which there were very few European plantations, whereas the northern part of the colony, in which lay the large plantation districts, as well as the chief centres for recruiting labourers, was completely free from the rebellion. At no time was the hut tax in German East Africa higher than in neighbouring Kenya, and it was levied with due consideration for the districts which were economically weak or backward, such as the region of the revolt. In reality, the revolt arose, as has been proved by ex-Governor Count Goetzen, through a movement which was spread by a native wizard. The revolt took its name from the water (Maji) which the magician carries as an aid to his spells. It is true that the crushing of this revolt entailed a relatively large sacrifice of native life, since the rebels, depending upon the efficacy of their magic talisman, revealed a most unusual degree of tenacity and contempt for death, just as the Soudanese dervishes against whom Kitchener fought did under frenzied psychic influences, with the same decimating results. But the suggestion that these losses were occasioned by cruelties on the part of the Germans is an unworthy fabrication.

In relation to the third revolt, that of **the Hereros in German South-West Africa,** this was occasioned through the gradual penetration of the white settlers, in whom the natives saw a menace to their continued possession of the land. In this respect it resembled the revolts with which white settlers had had to contend in North America, in Australia, and in South Africa. The Herero revolt began with a massacre of all German settlers who happened to fall into the hands of the rebels. The Herero developed unexpected powers of resistance, so that the despatch of considerable bodies of troops from Germany became necessary. They were defeated only after long and wearisome fighting, and it is true that a part of them fled into the sandy wastes, where they died of thirst.

The British Blue Book misrepresents the facts to such a degree as to make it appear that the Herero tribes had been persistently and cruelly oppressed by the German colonists and that the crushing of the rebellion had been a mere war of extermination. These charges have been completely refuted by the before-mentioned German White Book, which, nevertheless, does not attempt to conceal the fact that at times military methods were adopted in combating the revolt *which were not sanctioned by the German Government and were formally repudiated.* These measures may be explained, if not excused, by the bitterness occasioned by the massacre of the German settlers. Let it not be forgotten, however, that many a native tribe in the colonies of other nations has been almost or completely exterminated. We shall see how many of the Rifis of Morocco are left when France has completed her present work of "civilization" in that country.

There exists, however, the testimony of the Herero themselves, which goes to prove that the opinion of these natives with respect to German rule and German methods of warfare was and is in reality utterly different from that which the English Blue Book - intended as it was to prepare public opinion for the seizure of German South-West Africa - had concocted from all sorts of dubious sources. Such testimony exists not only in the form of utterances of Herero chieftains in the years following the war, but the funeral of the chief of the whole Herero peoples, Samuel Maharero, on August 26, 1923, took such a form that it amounted to a direct tribal manifestation in favour of Germany.[7] All the ceremonies, even to the smallest details, were modelled after the German pattern. The Herero came to the funeral almost to a man in German tropical uniform and in German colours. The German helmet of the Protectorate troops, with its black, white, and red cockade, was everywhere in evidence. Many Herero had sewn black crosses with white edges on their sleeves, and declared that these were meant to represent Iron Crosses. Several Herero declared to Germans who were present that they were also Germans, and wished to bury their chief with German honours. Can anyone imagine that the Herero would behave in this manner if they had been treated in any such fashion as the English Blue Book alleges and were filled with hatred for their former rulers? Would they not rather have sought to avoid everything which could remind them of the days of German rule?

It is not quite clear what can be meant by the charge of "arbitrary requisitioning" which is brought against the German colonial administration in the Note to the Versailles Treaty, and confusion in the mind of the prompters of the Note must be assumed. It may refer to the charge levelled in the Handbook and various official propagandist writings that the native police soldiery were allowed to have things their own way in their dealing with the other blacks and that they used this liberty for purposes of blackmail. The nature of the negro is such that cases of the abuse of authority by native police-soldiers or other officials will always occur wherever such men are immune from the direct supervision of their superiors. But it is absolutely untrue to say that this evil was encouraged, or even consciously tolerated, in the German colonies and that the negro was there allowed any kind of licence. On the contrary, when any such case of abuse of authority became known, the delinquent received exemplary punishment. Recognizing the danger of employing natives, even those with a record of many years' service, in independent positions, the German Government avoided it as much as possible. If, in spite of all these precautions, "arbitrary requisitioning" took place, it can only have been in isolated instances, and the culprits were clever enough to escape the attention of their superior officers. It is certain that such things have not occurred oftener in German Protectorate territory than in the colonies belonging to other nations.

In the various pamphlets directed against German colonization, great attention is devoted to the alleged excessive resort to judicial punishment by whipping. The whip or cane is used in all colonies where there are primitive races to deal with, the native territories under British and French rule not excepted.[8] It is really impossible to do without it altogether, for the native in many respects resembles a child. Efforts to substitute punishment by fines or imprisonment for whipping produced most discouraging results. The sharpest criticism of the use of the lash is always heard from those who have had no experience in dealing with primitive races and are inclined to apply to them the European standards proper for absolutely different conditions.

Whatever may be thought of punishment by whipping, however, it is a fact that Germany did not employ this measure more frequently than her neighbours. All nations are subject to the same social phenomenon, namely, that the first settlers in a new colony are men of abundant energy, without much understanding for the soul of the native. When these settlers receive positions, either official or private, which put them in command of a number of blacks, they are apt to exceed their authority, particularly in the matter of whipping. Germans make no attempt to conceal the fact that in the early years of their country's colonizing activity such cases of abuse occurred, and that an exact control by the higher authorities was rendered difficult, if not impossible, by the lack of means of transport. But this stage was left behind within a comparatively short time.

A report to the British Government from its Embassy in Berlin, written in 1894, barely ten years after Germany had acquired her colonies, stated:

> "The power of punishing their labourers is doubtless exercized by many masters, but it is never recognized by the German authorities, and complaints are often brought by the workmen to the courts, accusing the masters of ill-treating them, or of withholding their wages. These appeals for protection to the judicial authorities are rightly regarded as a great step in advance, and a special inspector has been appointed to look after the welfare of the poorer workpeople and to report any ill-treatment which may come under his notice. A few years ago no labourer would have dared to bring a civil or criminal action against his master, now they do so... a sure sign of the civilizing influence exercised by the Government and the missions over native public opinion"(p. 37).[9]

By way of contrast let the reader ask himself what was going on in the colonies of Belgium, to mention no others, at that time and far later.

It was precisely in relation to the punishment of the lash that both the Colonial Secretary in Berlin and the various Governors of the colonies laid particular weight upon most careful restrictions. So far as whipping was deemed unavoidable, all possible measures were taken for the protection of the natives, and any ill-treatment of natives by private persons was proceeded against with the utmost energy.

All these efforts were crowned with success. The conditions which prevailed in the German colonies in the years immediately preceding the war were by no means less favourable than those prevailing in similar colonies belonging to other nations. One important difference must be mentioned, and it is to Germany's credit. An accurate register was kept of all cases in which punishment by whipping had been inflicted in the German colonies, particularly since Secretary of State Bernhard

Dernburg, in 1907, issued more drastic orders for the protection of the natives in all the colonies. There were also other regulations to this end. The official who had ordered the punishment was obliged to be present in person, or to send a representative. In addition, a doctor or Red Cross official was obliged to be in attendance. This form of carrying out the punishment of whipping was naturally chosen in order that the negro might be protected in every way from abuse; yet in certain propagandist pamphlets the facts are so maliciously distorted that these supervisory measures are so represented as to suggest that brutal officials found pleasure in being present in order to contemplate and gloat on the sufferings of the prisoners! Such protective regulations are not found to the same extent in the colonies of other nations.

It would be a great mistake, however, to suppose that simply because the official German annual report contains careful statistics of the numbers of whippings inflicted (whereas no such statistics are to be found in the yearly reports of other colonies), there was little or no whipping in other colonies. My predecessor as Governor of German East Africa, Baron von Rechenberg, when travelling in British East Africa before the war, was shown the register of punishments in some of the principal towns of the colony (Nairobi, Mombasa, and Kisumu), and ascertained that many more natives were punished by whipping in that colony than in the neighbouring German colony, *but the British public could not know anything of this.* Moreover, in British East Africa whipping was not regarded as a punishment to be inflicted by a judge, but as a mere police measure which an official could employ with or without supervision as he thought best. Similar arrangements prevailed in other foreign colonies.

The natives in the German Protectorates were also protected against being whipped or otherwise ill-treated by European planters or their servants. Special Labour Commissioners were appointed who were entrusted to keep watch upon the conditions of employment.

The anti-German propagandism works itself up into a particularly violent state of righteous indignation when it reports that the Germans

GERMAN COLONIZATION PAST AND FUTURE

had also caused women to be whipped in the Cameroons and in German New Guinea. This is supposed to be a specially significant illustration of German methods with natives. As regards German New Guinea the accusation is simply false. In proof of it the Handbook cites the speech of the Social-Democratic Deputy Ledebour, delivered in the Reichstag on March 26, 1906. According to this, Herr Rose, the Commissioner of the Colonial Administration, who has spoken before Ledebour, had acknowledged the truth of the charge. Reference to the official shorthand reports of the Reichstag[10] shows that Herr Rose had done no such thing, but that Herr Ledebour had misunderstood him. The matter was cleared up at once by an interruption. In addition to this, anyone who examines these official shorthand reports will find that no one else had reported that women had been whipped in German New Guinea. In fact, this had never taken place in the colony.

In the Cameroons there was really one case of this kind. In 1893 a Herr Leist ordered some soldiers' native women followers to be whipped. An investigation followed, and this official was dismissed the service.

In so far as I myself have been able to ascertain, this is the only case of women having been condemned to whipping in any German colony. The whipping of women was strictly forbidden in all Protectorates. According to the regulations which had long been current, no sentence of whipping or beating might be passed against females of any age.

What is the state of affairs in other colonies? One would imagine, from the indignation aroused by the two isolated German cases, one of which, said to date from twenty years ago, is pure invention, while the other goes back thirty-two years, that such a thing as whipping native women was unknown elsewhere. In view of all that has been said against Germany, it is somewhat astonishing to read that to this day in the British colony of Nigeria, in the Mohammedan provinces ruled by an Emir, women are regularly whipped for breaking their marriage vows or for slander, and that the British Government raises no objection. The usual number of blows, dealt upon the back with a whip of rhinoceros hide, is one hundred. (In the German colonies the highest number of blows allowed to be dealt to a healthy full-grown man was twenty-five, which might not be repeated until two weeks later.) These facts are reported by the Governor of Nigeria himself, Sir Hugh Clifford, who made them public in a speech before the Council of Nigeria as late as December 29, 1920.[11]

The only reliable basis for forming a judgment as to whether the administration of justice is in accordance with the needs of the population is the degree of confidence reposed in it by the population - in this instance, the natives. In all parts of the German colonies the number of natives who voluntarily brought their disputes before a German court of law for settlement was continually on the increase, and the parties often came from long distances to seek justice. From a technical and legal point of view, there were, no doubt, many loopholes for criticism in the German method of doing justice. The procedure was not hedged about with all the formalities which are at once the guarantee and the hindrance of justice in the law of Europe, making every process a long and tiresome business, almost impossible for the poor man to undertake. The German method in the colonies was of a patriarchal character. The officials in charge were expected to use their knowledge of human nature and familiarity with native customs and usages rather than lose themselves and bewilder the litigants in the technicalities of a Europeanized procedure. But the method was independent and effectual. Although a Court of Appeal was lacking in most of the colonies, and only the more important judgments were laid before the Governor for ratification, the procedure was better fitted for the needs of the natives than a slow and complicated legal procedure would have been. I can speak with some experience, for I have myself administered justice in two colonies, and had the chief supervision of the law in a third. Various German judges, who also had seats in the Reichstag, fought for the introduction of a different system, but this opposition arose from a theoretical desire for legal correctness rather than from a practical knowledge of native needs.

It has been a favourite ground of complaint that German law in the colonies punished offences committed by blacks against whites more severely than those committed by whites against blacks. This phenomenon repeats itself in all colonies with a mixed population, and since the judges work independently, it is a matter in which the Government is practically powerless to interfere. Nevertheless, the colonial administrations did their best from the first to prevent inequality of justice, and so long [ago] as 1897 the British ambassador in Berlin (Sir Frank Lascelles) reported to Lord Salisbury:

> "The Imperial Chancellor has issued regulations by which strict conditions are laid down for the administration of justice by Europeans where natives are concerned, and there appears to be no room left for the abuses which had to come to light in former years. A further decree has settled the conditions under which contracts can be made with native labourers, in which every regard is paid to considerations of humanity. German and foreign authorities appear to agree as to the great progress made in the suppression of the abuses connected with slavery in German East Africa."[12]

Nor can it be said that white men's injustice was commoner in the German Protectorates than in those of other nations. One instance may suffice. The French Colonial Minister declared in the session of the French Chamber on December 21, 1922: "I know from personal experience that in the past the administration of justice was insufficient and inadequate when it came to the question of punishing crimes committed against the natives."[13] In the British colonies even to-day - particularly in Africa - there is also a great difference in the judgments passed by the courts upon blacks and whites. For Germany it can at least be said that the endeavours of her colonial administrators were always directed towards affording the natives every possible protection, even in such cases.

Further, the propagandist Handbook under criticism states that the chiefs in the German colonies were in general degraded to mere agents of the Government, and that all those who were not powerful enough to withstand the attacks of their masters were systematically ill-treated, whipped or imprisoned for trifling offences. This accusation cannot be better countered than by quoting the judgment of one of the most prominent, best informed, and most experienced of English colonial experts, the ex-Governor Sir Harry Johnston, who wrote of German East Africa during the war in the *Daily News:*

> "As a matter of fact, German rule, from the 'nineties right up to the outbreak of the war, was by no means unpopular in East Africa. The leading native chiefs were treated as we treat the Indian Rajahs, and the Arabs became so thoroughly reconciled to the German dominion that they became powerful allies of the Germans."[14]

Again, one may compare with this accusation an official British report on the Tanganyika Territory (German East Africa). In the first report, which covers the period from the conclusion of the Armistice to the end of 1920, there was an adverse criticism - premature, as will be seen - of the German system of *Akidas* (coloured district overseers), but in the second report, for the year 1921, we find the following conclusions:

> "The continuation of the German system of employing *Akidas,* paid native officials, has been fairly successful in the administration of the coastal districts. Here the tribes lack tribal organization and the *Akida* is generally connected with the people by descent. In up-country districts, where tribal cohesion is greater and where the *Akida* is often an alien, the policy has been to control the people through their own chieftains, replacing the *Akida* when possible by a headman of the people's choice."

This policy, even to the concluding words, coincides precisely with that followed by ourselves before the war in the districts in question in German East Africa.

The accusation of the degradation and ill-treatment of chiefs is no less untrue with respect to the other colonies. In the Cameroons, the Protectorate with the second largest population, it was the policy of the German administration, as clearly expressed in the Orders issued by the Governor to the local authorities, to strengthen the position of the chiefs, in order to rule the natives indirectly through their agency. This is *the exact opposite* of what the hateful propaganda of our enemies has declared to be the usage and the intent of German colonial policy.

The protest of the Akwa chiefs of the coast tribes of the Duala, of which much is made in the propagandist Handbooks, depended in the main upon the fact that in order to effect the necessary improvements in the most important seaport a partial sequestration of property and transplanting of the people had to take place. The resulting complaints aroused more attention than their importance merited, for they were brought before the Reichstag and the public in printed form before they had been examined and they thus furnished ready-made material for "colonial scandals." In the event a large proportion of the charges proved upon investigation to be absolutely unfounded, while all just complaints were remedied.

The real relations of the Cameroon chiefs to their German authorities have been clearly attested by the war, and also in part by later events. Almost without exception the chiefs and their people remained loyal to the German Government. When, after the gallant defence made by the Protectorate troops, these as well as the members of the Government were forced, under the pressure of the numerical superiority of the British and French troops, to beat a retreat into neutral Spanish territory, no fewer than 117 Cameroon chiefs, with their followers, accompanied them, refusing to desert the Germans. On February 2, 1919, these chiefs, then in Fernando Po, addressed a petition to the King of

Spain, begging him to use his influence at the conclusion of peace that they might continue to live under the German Government.[15]

Similar evidences of loyalty might be cited from Togoland; while the attitude of the headmen of the Herero in South-West Africa has already been mentioned.

Finally, with regard to the South Seas, it should scarcely be necessary to remind the reader of the excellent relations which obtained between the Samoan chiefs and the German Government. These chiefs sent a petition after the war to the King of England, begging to be freed from the Mandate government of the New Zealanders (see below). In German New Guinea, where a state of anarchy prevailed among the natives which prevented the establishment of any recognized chief, the Germans set in office chiefs of their own selection, and thereby successfully brought the natives themselves into play to help in bringing about orderly conditions.

I have no wish to exonerate or cloak any German who can be rightly accused of indefensible acts, and even if it were not dishonest so to do, it would be against my feeling of justice and seemliness, but the spokesmen of other countries must be equally honest and fair. The foregoing explanations and refutations, however, will have made it clear that the charges levelled against German colonial methods as a whole are baseless and mere fictions of the imagination. This cannot, unfortunately, be said of isolated cases, though even as to these a large part of the so-called facts paraded by the Handbook and other pamphlets are pure inventions, and this had been proved and acknowledged even at the time when these publications were written. Nevertheless, cases remain in which individual offenders were certainly guilty of ill-treatment of natives. Not even the progress of culture had been able to lighten the dark spots which lurk in human nature. Cases in which white men, pioneers of civilization, have degraded themselves by ill-treating the natives, fill the reader with regret and indignation. Such cases have occurred in the colonies of every nation, but if comparison be made with the proceedings of the Belgians and the French on the Congo,

Germany can claim that she has had far fewer cases of this kind than these colonizing nations. The great difference between the cases under German rule and similar cases under other nations is the extraordinary campaign against our colonies as such which was launched and joined in by certain of our parliamentary parties and their Press. In order to find instances of similar violent outbursts against colonial dignitaries to those which were levelled in the German Reichstag against Karl Peters, it is necessary to recall the time of Clive and Warren Hastings in English colonial history. It was only upon the young German beginner in colonization that malice concentrated its attention in the twentieth century. The older colonial nations had all had their dark "pasts," but time had charitably called oblivion upon them.

Roman Catholic Church at Lome, Togoland

Public school at Windhoek, South-West Africa

Native school at Malifa, Samoa

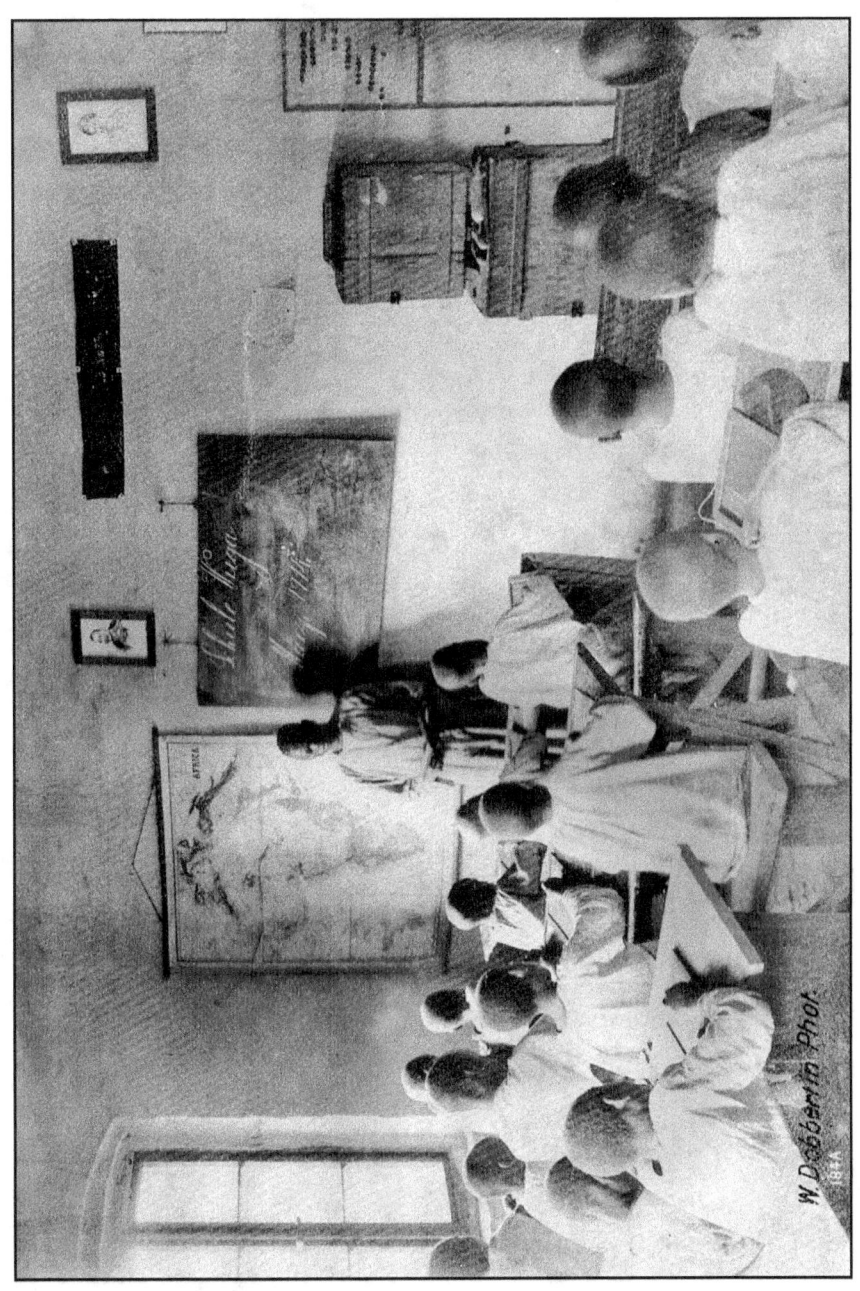

School at Wuga in Usambara, German East Africa

Carpenters' workshop, The Cameroons

8

The Question of Slavery and Forced Labour

It still remains to investigate the allegation that indefensible restrictions were imposed on the liberty of the natives in the German colonies. In the propaganda of our enemies the conditions are so depicted as to give the idea that the institution of slavery among the natives in those colonies, in contrast to all other colonies, had been retained and that the Germans had even introduced a kind of forced labour which practically amounted to a condition of serfdom.

It will suffice to establish a few facts in order to demolish the first of these two accusations - that pertaining to slavery. When Germany acquired her colonies the kidnapping of natives and the resulting trade in slaves were rampant in East as well as in West Africa. Both evils were abolished in the course of a few years through the energy and initiative of the German Government, though often only after stubborn struggles with the slave-dealers, especially in German East Africa through the suppression of the Arab revolt.

On the other hand, a certain mild form of peonage which pertained to certain of the colonies was not immediately abolished. This restraint was exercised solely in order to avoid too sudden changes and to prevent positive injury to the native population, as well as injustice to the old domestic serfs who were incapable of securing new employment, and for whom their existing masters were pledged to provide. Provision was, however, made for the gradual abolition of this form of house peonage. Thus all children born of domestic serfs after a certain date (December 31, 1905, in German East Africa) were declared to be legally free, and their liberation was greatly facilitated through purchase by the serfs themselves or through emancipation by the authorities. This in a comparatively short time would have led to the complete abolition of peonage. In spite of this the German Reichstag in 1912 passed a resolution that domestic peonage in German East Africa was to cease for good on January 1, 1920. The Colonial Office took measures for carrying out this decree and for protecting the masters and the serfs as far as possible from loss or damage. Had the World War not broken out, domestic peonage would have been abolished long before now.

In the light of these facts, it is wilful and ungenerous misrepresentation to describe (as has been done) the recent Ordinance of the British in Tanganyika Territory (that part of German East Africa which Great Britain demanded under the Mandates), to the effect that no person may hold another as a slave against his will, as "an act of emancipation" and "a great humanitarian measure" of which the Germans would never have been capable. Moreover, this Ordinance, as was pointed out by Mr. Grimshaw in his report as representative of the International Labour Commission to the Permanent Mandate Committee of the League of Nations, has a more negative than positive character, since it still permits the existence of a voluntary system of peonage.[1]

With regard to the other German colonies now in alien hands, the aforementioned report does not convey the impression that anything of importance has been altered with respect to the traces of peonage still existing in those regions. Particularly worthy of note are the observations made in the report (based on a summary of all the Mandate reports) to the effect that peonage did not necessarily imply a worse treatment of serfs than was likely in the freedom enjoyed in present economic conditions, and that the serfs themselves manifested no general desire for formal emancipation.

Here, again, it is possible to call the diplomatic representatives of Great Britain in Germany as witnesses in favour of our much-maligned colonial administration. Report after report sent to the British Foreign Office from the later years of last century (that is, ten or a dozen years after Germany began colonization) records the drastic measures taken for the suppression of slavery and the progress made in abolishing the milder institution of domestic serfage. Thus the British Embassy in Berlin reported in relation to East Africa in 1894:

> "It would appear that the German administration in East Africa has not interfered, to any great extent, with the prevailing customs in regard to domestic slavery, which is generally speaking of a mild form, and against which there is no movement amongst the slaves themselves. Domestic slaves are passed on from father to son, or to any lawful heir of the original owner. On the other hand, very stringent measures are taken to suppress slave raiding and dealing. Any Arabs or natives caught *flagrante delicto* are condemned to death."[2]

A report to the London Foreign Office on the Cameroons for 1897 stated:

> "Slavery has lost ground on the coast and so far as the power of the Government extends. The natives (and especially the Duallas) seem to adopt the point of view of Europeans in this respect with wonderful quickness, and as an instance may be cited the election of a former slave to the post of arbiter on the arbitration court composed of the most important of the Dualla chiefs."

Again, on the same colony it was reported in 1900:

> "Slavery has entirely disappeared in all the region immediately under German control, and it is stated that not a single case of

the sale or purchase of a slave from the interior of the Cameroons littoral has been noted between 1895 and 1899. The Government will not be able to entirely suppress the slave trade in the interior until the country has been subjugated."[3]

A later report on East Africa stated:

"The institution of slavery is, however, clearly dying out in German East Africa, and will disappear when the country is provided with better means of communication. A decree of the Imperial Chancellor issued in December, 1904, provides that all children of slaves born after December 31, 1905, are free."[4]

In these circumstances it is certainly difficult to justify any reproach being made against the German colonial administration for having gone carefully and gradually about the work of suppressing the remaining fragments of this mild form of serfdom, with a view to abolishing them with reasonable consideration for the ancient customs and existing economic needs of the natives. Besides, similar conditions prevailed in the colonies of other European Powers and are being gradually supplanted there in a precisely similar manner.

Those English critics who try to make out that Germany upheld slavery in her colonies might be well advised to remember the adage about stone-throwing in glass houses. Having defended my own Government against unjust and uncharitable aspersions, I am not unmindful that a British Government cannot always do at once all it might like in such a matter. Long after Germany had begun her earnest crusade against slavery in East Africa the practice continued in a British territory in that part of the continent. Sir Charles Eliot wrote in 1905, in his book *The East African Protectorate* (of which territory he was the British Administrator):

> "The position of our East African possessions with regard to slavery is somewhat peculiar. They are founded on the suppression of slavery... yet by a strange combination of circumstances the East African Protectorate is severely, and not altogether unjustly, criticized for maintaining and tolerating slavery at the present day. The facts of the case are that, owing to the promises which we made to the Arabs when we took over the coast, slavery is recognized as legal within the Sultan's (Zanzibar) dominions - that is, in a strip ten miles wide along the coast.... The contrast is certainly unfortunate, and illustrates what foreigners call our hypocrisy" (pp. 233-4).

I do not myself apply the hard word just quoted, but merely remind the reader that the best of Governments cannot always roughly override circumstances, but may have to tolerate evils longer than they wish from a fear of inducing worse ills by indiscriminate and precipitate action. It is equally justifiable to remind our critics that so late as 1921 slaves were allowed to be recaptured and re-enslaved within the precincts of the British Legation at Adis Abeba, the capital of Abyssinia, and that the British Foreign Office refrained from protests until the abuse became a public scandal. I quote from the reports of English eye-witnesses:

> "Abyssinia is the last home of open slavery. In its capital, Adis Abeba, there are more slaves than free men. The British Legation itself is full of slaves, owned by the Legation servants, who would not take service if they were not allowed to bring their chattels with them. The Legation compound is British soil, yet not only do slaves who enter it not become instantly free, but if they have escaped from their owners, their owners can and do enter it without hindrance to recapture them. That is an odd enough fact, but a still odder one is that a great many of these slaves are *British subjects captured by slave raids into British territory.*"

These writers continue:

> "Gangs of slaves, marching in misery, the men chained together in rows, and the women and children dragging themselves along beside the main body, can be seen by any traveller in Southern Abyssinia to-day. Some of these slaves are captured in Abyssinian territory, *others in British East Africa, others in Anglo-Egyptian Soudan.* One of the writers of these articles has seen with his own eyes a convoy of ten thousand slaves marching towards the great slave market of Jimma; and in the course of a single day's march along the trail he has counted the dead and dying bodies of more than fifty captives who have dropped by the roadside.... These things we have seen. And we have seen also hundreds of square miles of territory utterly depopulated by Abyssinian raids. Most of this territory is within the confines of the Abyssinian Empire, *but part of it is within the British Empire.* The facts are not unknown to the British Foreign Office."[5]

Remembering the revival, by English pamphleteers, of so many refuted and recanted slanders against German colonial administration, I would not suggest that the evils here spoken of have gone unremedied, though no later information is in my possession. The crucial point, however, is that while the seizure of Germany's colonies has been excused by what took place many years ago, the incidents and conditions above narrated refer to yesterday. It is equally pertinent to mention the later scandal of the sale of girls in Hong Kong which led to a protest conference in London in February, 1922. It was stated by the English Anti-Slavery Society that it was estimated that no fewer than 50,000 girls were at that time held in bondage in that British territory.

The most important publication with reference to the alleged existence of forced labour in the German colonies is the *Open Letter* addressed by Bishop Frank Weston, then of the English University Mission for Zanzibar and East Africa, to General Smuts. This letter was written during the war, and it was later included in the form of an appendix in the aforementioned collection of calumnies published by Evans Lewin. The title of the *Open Letter* in the English edition is "The Black Slaves of Prussia," and in the German edition "Das Martyrium der Eingeborenen" ("The Martyrdom of the Natives"). The Bishop himself has since explained to the world, in a booklet published in 1919 entitled *The Serfs of Great Britain,* being a sequel to "The Black Slaves of Prussia," how this document came to be published. In the course of this statement he says:

> "When I wrote my *Open Letter* to General Smuts, I called it 'Great Britain's Scrap of Paper: Will she honour it?' I was alluding to her promise of justice to the weaker peoples. *The Imperial Government took my letter, cut out some inconvenient passages, and published it under the title 'The Black Slaves of Prussia.'* I suggest that East Africans have now become 'The Black Serfs of Great Britain.'"

The reader is asked to weigh the words put in italics. They afford a not very creditable illustration of the way in which the nefarious propagandism aimed against Germany was machined.

The *Open Letter* contains a reproach against the German East African Government for having instituted forced labour. But both pamphlets show that the Bishop disagrees, for Christian and humane reasons, with the system followed by the British and Germans alike in the sphere of black labour. In the later pamphlet he attacks the British regulations issued in 1919 for Zanzibar and British East Africa, providing that there should be forced labour for public works and that work on private plantations should be furthered by semi-compulsion (sometimes euphemistically called "encouragement") of the natives. The Bishop makes this attack with the same energy which he expended in his first pamphlet upon the conditions in German East Africa, conditions which in his opinion amounted to forced labour. He says:

> "Great Britain is doing with its Africans what Lenin and Trotsky are said to do with the Russians. It is ordering a conscription of citizens for labour. Also, it is placing the resources of the Government at the service of a small band of European settlers."

These two extracts clearly show that the question at issue is essentially one of different points of view - the irresponsible personal and private view as opposed to the responsible official, the purely humanitarian and democratic view as opposed to the administrative and economic. The difference is explained by the fact that the humanitarian is free to advocate ideal theories, while the administrator has to pay regard to the actual facts and conditions of practical life as he finds them.

The English Bishop is opposed to any kind of forced labour for natives, whereas the administrations of all colonizing nations apply the principle of forced labour when public works are in question, and stimulate the natives in every practicable way to the performance of useful tasks. The principles followed in the German colonies were similar to those laid down on several occasions by Joseph Chamberlain, when Colonial Secretary. He stated in the House of Commons on August 6, 1901:

> "I believe it is good for the native to be industrious, and we must bend every effort to teach him to work.... There never was a people in the whole course of history which did not work. In the interests of the natives of all Africa, we must teach them to work."

Again, speaking in the same place on March 24, 1903, he said:

> "I continue to believe that under all circumstances the progress of the natives towards civilization is only secured when they shall be convinced of the necessity and dignity of labour; and therefore

I think that everything we can reasonably do to encourage the natives to work is highly desirable."

The part of Bishop Frank Weston's pamphlet against German East African administration which accuses the Germans of employing forced labour for private work and advances other allegations against them has been answered in a most convincing manner by Baron von Rechenberg, who was my immediate predecessor in German East Africa, in his pamphlet *German Colonial Policy before the Bar of the World* (1918, p. 36). Everyone in East Africa knows that Baron von Rechenberg, whom Bishop Weston himself in his pamphlet calls "one of the best and most humane functionaries," was the most active opponent of such forced labour during the whole of his six years of office in German East Africa - from 1906 to 1912. The Secretary of State for the Colonies also maintained his opposition, in the face of demands from various sides, against the natives being forced to work on the plantations. Regulations opposed to such demands, and definitely protecting the natives against forced labour, were actually put into effect. This action, however, did not interfere with the encouragement of the native to useful work and his receiving instruction to that end.

Curses have a strange way of coming home to roost. Here, again, it is easy to turn the tables upon our accusers. At the present time, as discussions in the British House of Commons and Government papers show, the white authorities and traders of British Kenya are hankering for forced labour for the plantations, and wish to get rid of the obligation to obtain the British Colonial Secretary's sanction to the same.[6] The Nairobi correspondent of *The Times* of July 30, 1925, reported that a number of natives who refused to work on a railway had been arrested and either fined or imprisoned. As the convictions were illegal, they were subsequently quashed and the fines were ordered to be returned, but there is no mention in the report of any compensation being paid to the natives who were wrongfully kept in prison for a fortnight before being tried. It is fair to add that the home Government has firmly insisted that the consent of the Colonial Secretary shall be obtained before "compulsory recruitment" (i.e. forced labour) can be resorted to, and has stipulated that such consent will only be given for specified works and for definite periods.[7]

How British settlers, living at present under the changed conditions in German East Africa, judge of German achievements in that colony as compared with those under the Mandate administration, is plainly to be seen from an article in the *Dar-es-Salam Times* of March 4, 1922. The passage runs as follows:

> "This journal has pointed out ad nauseam that the native cannot be expected to develop the country by himself. He needs European guidance and co-operation. One is forced to say that he was happiest when the Germans went in for agricultural enterprise and development, providing him with work, money and food, at the same time instructing those who were interested in more modern methods of agriculture than they had hitherto met with. *Since our occupation, agriculture has languished. European enterprise has been far from encouraged, and the result is a generally poverty-stricken and dissatisfied native populace.*"

In view of such impartial evidence, what answer is needed to the suggestion conveyed by the Note to the Versailles Treaty, that the various forms of forced labour (whether by themselves or in conjunction with the aforementioned "cruel oppressions" and "arbitrary requisitions" is not quite clear) have "depopulated wide stretches in East Africa," and also in the Cameroons, to which we shall return later? The principal witness cited in all these publications is a Dutch priest, Pater van der Burgt, who lived in the interior and complained that not a third of the labourers recruited for work on the plantations ever returned. The statement itself was justified. The cause, however, was not due to the depopulation of German East Africa through the death of the natives, but to the development of transport, trade, and agriculture. Many natives preferred to live in the settled localities near the railway or larger settlements, rather than in their remote original homes, to be reached only after weeks of marching. But now mark the sequel. The same Pater van der Burgt, in an interview on November 11, 1918, repudiated the false ideas and impressions which had been artificially created by tearing a few of his sentences from their context.[8] He then formulated his judgment thus: "German colonization in German East Africa was the greatest of blessings both for the country and the people." He also declared that the terms made use of by the official anti-German propagandists, such as "modern slavery," "forced labour," and so on, were fraudulent. Yet - will it be credited? - *not one of the writers or publishers of the pamphlets in which an attempt is made to justify the violent filching of the German colonies has mentioned in any later edition this repudiation of the Pater's.* It is by such suppression of facts that this cruel wrong has been done to Germany.

The fact is that there exists no evidence at all to show that any decrease of the native population has occurred under German rule in German East Africa. I myself regard any such decrease as highly improbable, and I base my opinion upon a knowledge of the native population gained in the course of frequent journeys to and fro over almost the entire territory. The blacks of East Africa are in the main a strong and virile race. The conditions which formerly caused such great mortality had practically ceased to exist under German rule. The constant internecine feuds of the tribes had ceased. Plagues, such as smallpox, which formerly carried off the greatest number of victims, had been effectually combated; and when a famine happened to occur, the administration was at once at hand with relief measures. The native labourers were protected in an ever-growing degree by splendid sanitary arrangements and hospitals well staffed with skilled German doctors and attendants. Instead of decreasing, it is probable that the native population was on the increase during the years preceding the war. It is impossible to furnish definite proof of this, since the census had not been taken with any great accuracy. It was only after the war had been illegally carried into the colonies, in violation of the Congo Act, that the negroes of German East Africa began to suffer serious losses. These were occasioned directly by fighting and privation, but also indirectly, and probably to a far greater extent, through the outbreak of plagues and pestilence, due to the enforced cessation of all the preventive and sanitary measures which had been applied by the Germans with such notable success.

In the Cameroons the Germans are also reproached for having, as is alleged, caused a decimation of the population through forced labour. This charge likewise is absolutely unwarranted. Forced labour was employed in the Cameroons, just as in the other colonies, only when it was a question of executing public works. For all other undertakings volunteers, who were recruited by private agents, were employed. In the propagandist booklets, much is made of the comparatively high mortality rate on certain plantations. It is true that the death-rate among the native labourers was at times regrettably high. The reason for this was twofold. In the first place, most of the plantations were situated in the unhealthy coast regions of the Cameroons, where epidemics were frequent, and secondly, when natives from the high-lying, healthy regions in the interior were employed, they fell easy victims to the fevers prevailing in the low-lying districts. Similar experiences were made in other colonies - not only in the German territories, but wherever the experiment was tried of utilizing natives from the higher regions in the climatically more unfavourable plantations. Here let it be said in passing that the Report of the Permanent Mandates Commission of the League of Nations clearly shows that even under the present Mandate government of the German colonies similar regrettable results have followed upon attempts made to transplant the native workers from their homes to regions with different climatic conditions.[9] It should be noted, however, that in the Cameroons in particular extraordinary efforts had been made in the matter of caring for the health of the native labourers. Hospitals and doctors were there in abundance; and regulations for the well-being of the natives had been issued, obliging the larger European plantations to make sufficient medical provision in proportion to the number of workmen employed, including a staff of trained hospital attendants.

The apparent depopulation of certain districts in the Cameroons was due, not to work on the plantations, but to another cause altogether. Whether the propagandists who were directed to defend the annexation of the German colonies by pamphlets knew the actual facts or not I cannot say, but if they did not the immorality of employing ignorant writers in such an agitation is self-evident. The actual cause was the exploitation of the wild-rubber trees growing in one part of the colony. This exploitation led to undue demands being made upon the natives living on or near the caravan routes affected. These men were required as carriers and also to attend to the needs of passing caravans, and this work engaged them to such a degree as to threaten their family life. The result was that the natives sought to avoid the constant disturbances and the work caused by the passing caravans by moving away from the neighbourhood. These then tended to become deserts, not on account of the population dying off, but on account of it moving away. The German colonial administration was decidedly opposed to these abuses and had taken measures designed to place the economic existence and family life of the natives on a securer basis than that afforded by the exploitation of the wild rubber. In any case, as the supply of wild rubber was gradually becoming exhausted, the exploitation of the rubber could not be a permanent occupation.

It is certainly true that this exploitation, with the accompanying effects of a tremendous growth of the caravan service and of the demand for carriers, was at times a severe burden to a part of the native population. Yet the administration did all in its power to remedy and alleviate the evil and find other employment for the blacks.

If the wild-rubber districts of the Cameroons be compared with the wild-rubber districts of other West African colonies, the German colony gains greatly by the comparison. No one ever heard of "red rubber" in the German colonies, nor of forcing the natives by means of bloody outrages to deliver ever larger quantities of the coveted rubber. No black was ever murdered or crippled in the Cameroons, as were hundreds in the Congo regions, simply because the hapless wretches did not supply sufficient rubber to their avaricious masters. In the German colonies, in a word, there were none of the atrocities which were perpetrated for years in the neighbouring French and Belgian territories until the conscience of the entire civilized world demanded their cessation. Yet to-day France and Belgium are in possession of German territories in virtue of violent seizure and in violation of the conditions of peace accepted by Germany at the instance of the American Government.

What has been said of German East Africa with respect to the alleged depopulation applies no less to the Cameroons. The native population trekked from one region to another. Any general decrease in the sum total of the population, however, cannot be proved and it is also highly improbable. According to the observations and notes made by the last Governor of the Cameroons, Governor Ebermaier, in the course of his many journeys through the colony, it may be asserted with certainty that the number of natives in the Cameroons immediately before the war was considerably higher than had been stated in former official reports. The losses occasioned in the territory by the war and the serious disadvantages caused by the absence of the German measures for combating disease and pestilence have not been remedied by the Mandate Government, which can show nothing comparable to the efficient German medical organization, as is frankly admitted by visitors to the colony.

Some more specific observations must be added regarding the labour conditions in the German colonies under Mandate administration. The first thing that must be made clear is that the system of forced labour for public works *has been retained everywhere.* The reports to the League of Nations of the Mandate Governments between which the Cameroons have been divided, i.e. those of France and Great Britain, contain some remarkable statements as to labour conditions. The French report calls attention to the fact that in the French section of the Cameroons certain difficulties arise because "the natives of Equatorial Africa neither feel the need for work nor the wish to work, nor have they any taste for it."

The separate reports upon the same tribe in the British section of the colony reveal quite a different aspect. There "the continued operation of the large European plantations is secured in a most satisfactory way by more than 10,000 labourers, who keep the work going by their own efforts.... Not one of these labourers is bound by a long-term contract, or indeed by a contract of any kind. On the contrary, each is free to go away when he chooses."[10] It is scarcely necessary to point out that the arbitrary frontier division between the British and French sections, a frontier line which divides tribes in two, cannot be the cause of such a totally divergent attitude of the natives towards their work. The "joy in work" displayed by the 10,000 labourers in the second report can be explained only by the employment of some means, not mentioned in the text, of making labour appear desirable to the negroes.

It should also be remarked as to the French part of the Cameroons that apart from the compulsory military service now introduced therein, as already mentioned, and the employment of soldiers for service outside the colony, the lot of the natives under the French Mandate was rendered considerably more unfavourable by the circumstance that according to the French official report for 1921[11] the recruiting of labourers for undertakings outside the territory is granted if the permission of the head of the territory is obtained. Thus it becomes possible for the French to utilize natives from the Cameroons for the unhealthy territories, with deplorable sanitary conditions, which are owned by French concessionary companies in the regions of the Congo and the Ubangi.

It should be added that the League of Nations Secretariate published in the present year (1925) the report of a Committee which had been appointed to investigate the subject of slavery. In this document it is stated that serfdom still prevails in the French colonies of tropical Africa as well as in the British possessions of Burma and Assam. Yet the Committee "hesitates, for economic reasons, to recommend the compulsory liberation of all serfs," and only proposes that serfdom should be declared to have no legal status and serfs be able to free themselves, if they wished, without expense. The Committee even defends the employment of forced labour on public works and the coercion of the native labourer to work as an "educative measure." How weak and apologetic such recommendations look when compared with the mock morality of the accusations made during the war against Germany in regard to both these questions, on which she had already gone farther in her colonies than the League of Nations and some of her accusers are prepared to go even to-day!

Farm at Wuga in Usambara, German East Africa

Coconut plantation, German East Africa

Young sisal plantation, German East Africa

Preparing sisal, German East Africa

9

German Rule and Mandate Rule Compared

Hitherto attention has been concentrated upon the more negative aspects of the question at issue, since it was necessary to rebut baseless charges, adjust false perspectives, put questions in a right and true light, and correct misrepresentations generally - misrepresentations due sometimes, no doubt, to pure though culpable ignorance, but more often, it is to be feared, to malice and a wish to deceive. To say all that would be possible and justifiable on the positive side of the question would entail the writing of a whole series of books on German administration and what it has done for territories redeemed from conditions of disorder, violence and savagery. Here no more than the merest outline of the full story can be given.

I. The Germans as Pioneers of Civilization

After all, the best answer to the accusations made against the Germans in the Covering Note of the Treaty of Versailles is to point to their more outstanding achievements in the development and civilization of the colonies before the war - achievements which were often of the greatest importance for the colonies of all nations. Names like those of Nachtigal, Schweinfurth, Wissmann, Emin Pasha, Stuhlmann, Baumann, Hans Meyer, Kandt, Count Goetzen, and Duke Adolf Friedrich of Mecklenburg are known and respected in expert colonial circles everywhere. It would be easy, however, to make the list twice as long, in order to show how great a share has been taken by German explorers and *savants* in the scientific exploration of the Dark Continent. In all branches of science and knowledge - in ethnology, philology, botany, zoology, etc. - are encountered the names and the discoveries of German scholars, missionaries, and travellers. No one has paid a more generous tribute to the achievements of the German colonial explorers, discoverers, pioneers, and scientists than the distinguished English authority Sir Harry Johnston in his books on Africa. I mention only his *Opening up of Africa,* published in 1911 (see pp. 238-41). A recent very characteristic example of the real understanding and love for the peoples entrusted to his care which filled the soul of many a German official is the collection of Samoan proverbs published by the last Governor of Samoa, Dr. Erich Schultz, in the *Süddeutsche Monatshefte* for March, 1914.

But the greatest claim to fame which can be made by colonial Germans lies in the realm of medicine and hygiene, and particularly in the fight against the tropical diseases and plagues that beset white men, black men, and beasts alike, in the regions in which they have spent health, strength, and often life itself.

Nearly thirty years ago the British Foreign Office began to recognize and praise the scientific work done in the German colonies at the instigation of a Government and nation now declared to be unfit to colonize. Thus a report of that Office on East Africa (C 8649-3) for 1897 stated:

> "Progress has been made in scientific work, both in the way of exploration and medical, botanical, and geological research. It may be confidently hoped that the results of the inquiries now zealously conducted in the German colonial establishments will be to add to the world's knowledge as to the hygienic conditions

of life in tropical climates and the method of cultivation of tropical plants."

Many such tributes were paid in later years both in British official reports and in those of scientific investigators and travellers. It was the great German scientist Robert Koch who, in the course of repeated sojourns in British and German colonies, made such epoch-making discoveries and laid the foundations for the extirpation of various scourges. The blessings which this man and other German scientists and doctors after him have conferred on the tropical colonies - and by no means only German colonies - by their successful methods of combating disease are beyond calculation. I need only remind the reader of the discovery of the Cholera Bacillus and of the resulting battle against Cholera in India and of the organization undertaken for the fight against the Sleeping Sickness, the Rinderpest and other plagues in Africa. Many scourges which formerly afflicted the native population and exacted a terrible death-rate - for example, Smallpox, have almost lost their significance in the German colonies, thanks to the unremitting labour of German science, both theoretical and practical. Other diseases, against which the natives were formerly entirely helpless, such as Framboesia and Syphilis, have been successfully cured since the discovery of Salvarsan.

It is a satire upon justice and a reproach to civilization that at the present time German scientists are obliged to engage in investigating pathological problems, of vital interest to the human race, in territories under alien rule on sufferance owing to the closure of our own Protectorates to them. For despite the seizure of the German colonies, the German zest for discovering new methods to combat disease continues unabated. In Germanine (Bayer 205) Germany has now discovered a certain remedy against the deadly Sleeping Sickness. At the moment of writing, a German expedition under the leadership of Professor Dr. Kleine, which had been two years in the British and Belgian colonies in Central Africa in order to test the efficacy of this remedy, has just returned home. Professor Kleine has established with certainty, by means of a great number of cases, that this remedy is capable of quickly and permanently curing this terrible scourge. This not only means salvation for the unfortunate mortals cursed with the Sleeping Sickness, who have hitherto been doomed to long suffering and generally to death, but it also signifies the restoration to life and economic activity of great districts in which the native population was dying out. The effects of this remedy have also been very favourable in the case of combating the bacillus of the illness induced by the tsetse fly. Whilst not as yet so auspicious as in the case of the Sleeping Sickness, there are many indications to prove that this German remedy will also succeed in ridding Africa of this second scourge - a prospect which opens up enormous vistas for the social and economic improvement of a great part of the Dark Continent. I may also mention Dr. Albert Schweitzer, who has already done so important and noble a work of research in Central Africa in connexion with the cure of Leprosy as well as Sleeping Sickness, as many distinguished Englishmen well know.

It is a matter beyond dispute that the scientists of no other civilized country have done so much by means of discoveries and the organized fighting of diseases and plagues as those of Germany. In view of facts such as these, what name should be given to that spirit of defamation, so unworthy and so unmanly, which still persists in declaring that the Germans have been failures in the field of colonial civilization?

It is a singular tribute to German scientific eminence and worth in the domain of tropical hygiene and medicine that there were English writers who called upon their Government to require from Germany, as one of the penalties of defeat in war, that she should communicate to other countries the pathological discoveries made by her great investigators and practitioners.

The enormous development of the German colonies during the short period of thirty years which elapsed between their acquisition and the outbreak of the war had impressed and astonished every traveller and scientist who had the opportunity of visiting them. Where there was formerly nothing but wilderness, interrupted merely by thinly populated native settlements, flourishing plantations had arisen producing, under European supervision, important values for the markets of the world.

Vast regions of bush, formerly devoid of all human life, had given place to farms, with their ever-increasing herds of cattle. Where a few precious products had aforetime been carried to the coasts by caravan for weeks and months on the heads of carriers, where dense jungles made advance almost impossible, where sand-dunes and deserts with their burning wastes scarcely permitted traffic even by ox-team, spick-and-span modern railways offered quick and safe communication between distant points, opening up great hinterlands, and enabling the tribes of the interior to emerge from their seclusion and participate in the great tasks of economic development.

Coast settlements which at the most were tiny villages when the German flag was hoisted had grown into modern towns, which were taking an ever-increasing part in world commerce. Wherever the traveller turned, whether to Tsing-tao in China, to Dar-es-Salam in German East Africa, or to any of the other neat and orderly seaports in the German colonies, there he was sure to find fine, well-planned and well-built towns which more than held their own with similar towns in alien colonies. The same may be said of the German railways and arrangements for traffic, of the plantations, and of the entire German colonial administration.

German solicitude for the health of the natives did not confine itself to the warfare against the diseases that afflicted man and beast, as above mentioned. Every care was also taken for the individual treatment of sick natives. Doctors, specially trained at home in the treatment of tropical diseases, devoted themselves to the care of the native communities, and their numbers grew from year to year. A considerable number of native hospitals were already in existence for the care of those suffering from serious maladies, and others were constantly being added. Minor cases were treated free in the polyclinics, and the natives made much use of these benefits. In all German colonies large sums of money were set apart for the medical needs of the natives, and provision was made for the free use of the expensive new remedies for tropical diseases. British military and other officers who have made acquaintance with the German colonies since 1914 have referred in terms of amazement and admiration to the remarkable work of their predecessors in town building, and have recommended German achievements in this sphere for imitation by their countrymen. No less warmly have British medical practitioners spoken of the wonderful hospitals and the hygienic service established by Germany in her oversea territories.[1]

A great work has been accomplished in the training of the natives to regular labour, while schools for artisans have disseminated useful technical knowledge and afforded them the opportunity of learning and following crafts and trades. It is a high compliment to German efficiency that when the British occupied German East Africa they found it expedient to transplant native artisans, trained under German auspices, into the adjacent British colony, to instruct the more backward natives there.

Agricultural schools have likewise extended the knowledge of modern and progressive forming methods, and enabled the natives to cultivate many new and profitable crops. The schools for the scientific study of cotton and other tropical plants which had been established in some of the colonies were also proving of great use and value to the natives.

In all the colonies, too, great concern was shown for the spiritual welfare of the natives. Numerous missionaries of the two great branches of the Christian religion were occupied in evangelizing the native population, which for the greater part was found sunk in the darkest heathenism. Many schools, Government as well as mission schools, were devoted to the education of the natives. Yet even our self-sacrificing missionaries have not been spared abuse. They are said to be guilty of political propagandism. But how and where? If they represented German national interests in German colonies, they were in the right. To say that they sought to prejudice the natives against their masters in British territories is to make a charge that cannot be substantiated.

In fairness to these devoted men I must cite in their favour two recent unbiassed testimonies, one from an English and the other from an American source.

Dr. Frank Lenwood, one of the leading officials of the London Missionary Society, in a letter to *The Challenge* of May 10, 1918, stated:

> "I am driven to the conclusion that the charges against them are due to suspicions, natural enough in war-time, but without real foundation, and that the statement has been repeated so often upon scanty evidence that it has come to be accepted as a fact. The great and unselfish service of German missions under the British flag calls for an impartial scrutiny of any statement made against them."

The Rev. Cornelius H. Patton, D.D., Corresponding Secretary of the American Board of Commissioners for Foreign Missions, stated at the Africa Conference held in New York City in November, 1917:

> "Africa cannot afford to lose the help of the German societies which were established in various parts of the continent before the war. The German missions in Togoland, in the north part of Cameroon, in German South-West Africa, and in German East Africa were being blessed of God in signal ways. They were making a unique contribution to Africa's evangelization and civilization. Their missionaries were second to none in self-sacrifice and zeal. Whatever geographical and governmental changes may occur, it will be nothing less than a calamity to the Kingdom of God if the Christian people of Germany are to have no further part in Africa's redemption."

The perils which European civilization entails for the primitive races in many ways were forestalled in the German colonies by a number of wholesome regulations. Trading in firearms was forbidden to natives and was in general subjected to a rigorous supervision. The sale of alcohol to natives was entirely prohibited in certain colonies, such as German East Africa and the South Sea Islands, while in the other colonies measures had been taken in accordance with international agreements to reduce to a minimum the danger arising from the use of alcohol. The natives were also protected against exploitation by Europeans through the provision that all contracts between whites and natives were subject to official approval, and that any attempt at evasion rendered the contract invalid. Land commissions or other authorities took care that wherever a sale of land by natives to whites took place sufficient acreage was left to the natives resident in the neighbourhood, and for their progeny. The impartial justice meted by the German officials gave the natives efficient protection from wrong and damage whether from whites or from fellow-blacks. The object constantly kept in view was the conservation of the health and bodily welfare of the labourers and their protection against exploitation.

It has been clearly shown that the seizure and partition of the German colonies were in no way justified by the slanders which were invented and disseminated for the simple purpose of giving to these acts the force of a specious moral sanction. This fact became evident soon after the booty in the shape of Mandates had been divided out, and it became clear that the mandatories were proving incapable of maintaining these colonies at the high level set by the Germans.

Thus Mr. Winston Churchill, when British Secretary for the Colonies, stated before the Imperial Conference on June 21, 1921, in relation to **German East Africa (Tanganyika):**

> "We have endeavoured to equip it with a government not inferior to the German administration which it had replaced... I am afraid that in a year or two the state of this Tanganyika Territory will compare unfavourably with its progress and prosperity when it was in the hands of our late opponents."[2]

This prophecy has been fulfilled in a startling manner, for conditions in German East Africa became most doleful, as will be shown in later pages.

Further, Mr. Ormsby Gore, the British Under-Secretary for the Colonies, stated in the House of Commons on July 25, 1923, apropos of the same German colony:

> "The mere fact that propaganda is still going on in Germany makes it absolutely incumbent upon us to give that vast territory, which in area is larger than Nigeria, and contains a population just over 4,000,000, at least as good and complete an administration as was given by the Germans in that country before the war."[3]

The British report upon the Cameroons for 1921 speaks thus of the German plantations there:

> "As a whole they are wonderful examples of industry, based on solid scientific knowledge."[4]

The same report goes on to say:

> "Apart from the regular employment afforded, the natives have been taught discipline and have come to realize what can be achieved by industry. Every labourer is an embryo planter. Large numbers who return to their villages take up cocoa or other cultivation on their own account, thus increasing the general prosperity of the country."[5]

Finally, as to German South-West Africa General Smuts, whom everyone will allow to possess exceptional experience in colonial matters, referred to the Germans, in a speech made in that Protectorate on September 16, 1920, as splendid colonists who fully deserved the

Government's support and encouragement.[6] Later he wrote to Privy Councillor Herr de Haas, a high functionary of the German Foreign Office, who was then in London:

> "The Germans settled at various times in various parts of the Union form one of the most valuable portions of our South African people. And I feel sure that the Germans of South-West Africa, whose successful and conscientious work in the territory I highly appreciate, will materially help in building up an enduring European civilization on the African Continent, which is the main task of the Union" (letter of October 23, 1923).

It is a simple act of justice to say that it was only in the Union of South Africa that a humane policy, and one in accordance with international law, was followed in the treatment of German subjects after the war. The Government of that Dominion refrained from beggaring the Germans of the South-West by expropriating their property without compensation, and even the concessions to which titles could be established were respected. It redounds to the honour of British and Dutch South Africans that when General Smuts announced to the Cape Town House of Assembly the decision so to act his words were "received with repeated cheers from all sections of the House."[7]

Considering the peculiar psychology of the French, it is difficult to conceive of their giving credit to German achievements of any kind. Nevertheless, even the French official Mandate reports cannot entirely suppress a certain recognition of what the Germans accomplished in the field of sanitation. The first of these reports states:

> "It is absolutely indisputable that the Germans in the Cameroons had begun a great undertaking in the matter of medical assistance, and that this had begun to bear its benevolent fruits."[8]

A later report (1921) concedes that "no inconsiderable results had been attained in this direction."[9] Further, a French newspaper wrote as follows in August, 1923, regarding the colonial activity of Germany in West Africa:

> "If all French colonies were equipped like the Cameroons and Togoland, a great step forward in their profitable development would be achieved. France, in all circumstances, must not fail to improve that which the Germans had already realized in their colonial territories as early as 1913."[10]

II. What the Mandatory Powers Have Achieved

The first achievement of the Mandatory Powers which accepted the office of administering the former German colonies on behalf of the League of Nations was that they laid down arbitrary frontiers in various colonies, so dividing tribes which were naturally homogeneous. As has been made plain in earlier chapters of this book, the partition of the colonies was not undertaken in any degree whatever from the point of view of the welfare of the natives concerned. On the contrary, the only consideration was to possess them and to do it with as little show of scheming, selfishness, and cupidity as possible. It has also been shown that in some cases the division was simply a realization of earlier agreements concluded secretly and never divulged to the world. The consequence is that in the West African colonies of the **Cameroons** and **Togoland,** which were divided between France and Great Britain, the tribes have been violently torn apart. In Togoland this has happened to the tribes of the Ewe, the Konkomba, and the Tschokossi. In the Cameroons, according to the official British report, a tract of "no-man's land " had been left on the frontier between the two spheres of influence, and this had become a refuge for criminal elements. The final delimitation has now done away with this evil, but nothing whatever has been heard of any action being taken by the mandatories to counteract the disastrous effects of the arbitrary determination of the frontiers.

The position created in the interior of **German East Africa** is much worse. Here the sultanates of Ruanda and Urundi were divided from the great mass of the German colony, which fell to the British share, and they were declared to be Belgian mandatory territory. Out of regard for the British lines of communication, however, an artificial frontier had been created, cutting off a large tract of the sultanate of Ruanda. King Msinga and his Watussi were seriously injured by this manoeuvre, their economic existence being actually jeopardized. The matter was brought to the notice of the League of Nations, upon which the British Government agreed to a revision of the frontier line, and thus the sultanate of Ruanda recovered the strip of territory which had been torn from it. But the fact remains that the sultanates of Ruanda and Urundi have been forcibly torn from German East Africa and incorporated in the Belgian Congo. This is a great economic disadvantage for the inhabitants of these two countries, since all their natural connexions are in the territory now under British rule.

The reports which the Mandatory Governments present annually to the Permanent Mandates Commission of the League of Nations in Geneva do not as a rule contain anything unfavourable to mandatory administration. From other communications, however, particularly those which have appeared in trustworthy British newspapers and other publications, it is clear that conditions are by no means so rosy as they have been officially represented to be.

Three detailed articles in the "Trade and Engineering Supplement" of *The Times*, the last in the issue of July 30, 1923, deal with the British mandated territory of German East Africa. In these articles the territory in question is referred to as a "bureaucrats' paradise." It appears that the administration employs far more officials than the German pre-war administration, and that the official corps can only be described as a tax-collecting organization; yet, notwithstanding that the heavy taxation imposed on the natives compels them to sell their cattle in order to meet their dues, so that they have sunk into a state of acute poverty, the administration cannot make both ends meet without considerable contributions from the British taxpayers at home. The condition of the colony in general has been described as deplorable. That these opinions are shared by the British living in the colony is plain from extracts from the local Press.[11]

Other extracts show that in April, 1923, in consequence of the exorbitant taxation, all the Arab and Indian traders had closed their shops, thereby causing serious difficulty in supplying the natives with provisions. Further, the Government procedure had called forth unanimous protest both from Europeans and coloured inhabitants.[12] It is stated that since the expulsion of the Germans the plantations of rubber, sisal hemp, etc., which had been brought to a high state of cultivation by the German planters, have for the greater part reverted to wilderness; the natives have less opportunity of earning money; and the pressure of taxation has increased.

On the latter point I quote from the Tanganyika correspondent of *The Times:*

> "The present scale of native taxation is a considerable hardship, at a time when the natives have little or no means of earning anything. It is surely wrong that natives should have to sell their cattle at a time when there is no demand for the purpose of raising the money necessary to satisfy the hut tax."[13]

With regard to the fight against disease, hygienic measures generally for the natives, and school instruction, the British Mandate Government, as may be seen from the details given in the official British annual reports on these matters, has not been able to reach anything like the standard achieved under the former German administration.

In the Cameroons and Togoland no less the expulsion of the German planters and traders has similarly led to serious economic results, both in British and French mandated territory. Many of the plantations have been thrown out of cultivation. In the French Cameroons no attempt is made to keep them up, and they are necessarily falling into ruin. In consequence of the reduced possibilities of earning a livelihood, the natives are much worse off than formerly. The entire stoppage of the German hospital service for the prevention and cure of epidemics, which was organized on a most lavish scale, is severely felt by the natives, particularly the lack of measures against Sleeping Sickness. The French have nothing similar with which to replace these German relief organizations, as may be seen from their own official annual reports. One of their chief troubles is the lack of trained doctors and assistants, of whom the German administration had always as many as it needed.

In French Togoland confusion and disorder have reigned under Mandate government from the first. Early in 1921 two English travellers, Marjorie and Alan Lethbridge, writing in the *Daily Telegraph* of their experiences in West Africa, referred unfavourably to the French occupation of the country. The French, they said, had no right to the country, and the subjected tribes would rather be under German rule as before than be forced to serve the French, whom they neither liked nor understood. Mention must also be made of the scandalous frauds by a Commissioner and other high officials in connexion with the confiscated German plantations. In the course of the investigations one of the officials implicated committed suicide and Commissioner Woelfell was recalled. According to the *Dépêche Coloniale et Maritime* of May 12, 1923, this man left the colony in a state of absolute disorder.

A newspaper circulating in the neighbouring British Gold Coast Colony writes as follows respecting the condition of the natives in French Togoland:

> "In every household, in the streets, you hear people murmuring and complaining of the exorbitant charges of the customs, licences, and taxes of various kinds levied by the French."[14]

A Togoland negro expresses himself still more drastically in a letter:

"The present Government is a misfortune for Togoland. They are like wolves. Everything is taxed three times over. Matters grow worse from day to day."

Another disadvantage to the natives in the territory under French administration, which includes the greater part of the two German West African colonies, is that owing to the militarization of the colony, now introduced, they are liable to be used for military service outside their homeland.

With regard to the South Sea colonies, I will only refer to **Samoa** and **German New Guinea.** Samoa, the "pearl of the South Seas," must be included in order to tell of the tragic fate that has overtaken its inhabitants, one of the most amiable populations on earth. This tragedy is a direct result of the incapable Mandate administration of New Zealand. The *Chicago Daily Tribune* of September 22, 1920, drew attention to the signs of retrogression and decay which had already overspread the colony since the Government of New Zealand took over the administration: though taxation had become intolerable, everything was falling into ruin; large plantations had been allowed to become desert, and the pineapple industry had been destroyed; while the treatment of the expelled Germans was described as barbarous.

The *Brisbane Daily Mail,* in February, 1921, likewise condemned the harrying out of the island of the German planters and their replacement by inexperienced men as a fatal blunder, and reported that the inhabitants were burdened by taxation, the only people who benefited being a crowd of officials of all kinds. The result was general discontent on the part of the Europeans and natives equally. In an article entitled "Who said Humanity?" the former American Consul at Apia has also testified to the cruel eviction of the Germans, whom he knew as industrious and efficient men, and told how the grateful natives assembled to witness their departure.

Further, during the war the dreaded Spanish influenza was by some means introduced into the colony, and in consequence of the incapacity of the New Zealand authorities, it spread to such an extent that one-fourth of the population are reported to have died of it. Here the Mandate administration has fallen short in nearly every direction, so that the old inhabitants, the British and other white settlers and the Samoans alike, have protested in equally strong terms.

Reference to **German New Guinea** is the more pertinent since here the contrast between appearances and facts is particularly crass. The make-believe of a successful Mandate administration assiduously engaged in developing the country, as would appear from reports sent to the League of Nations, and from other official publications, is contradicted by the dismal reality of decay, disaster, and false methods of government, of which abundant evidence comes from undeniably reliable sources. By the Treaty of Versailles the Allied Powers took the right, in defiance of international law, to appropriate the private property of Germans in all the colonies, and the Australian Government enforced this "right" in German New Guinea with great cruelty. From the time the colony was occupied by Australian troops until two years after the Armistice the German planters and merchants were allowed, and even encouraged, to carry on their plantation and commercial enterprises as usual. This they did with great zeal, seeking relief in that trying time of strain and suspense by redoubled energy and concentration upon their work; new plantations were laid down, and other developments and improvements carried out. Then just before Christmas of 1920 three vessels laden with young returned soldiers were landed on the island, and without notice or respite of any kind the Germans were ejected from their properties and turned out of their homes, and the totally inexperienced new-comers were at once put in charge as factors. Most of the evicted Germans were deported, being chiefly shipped to Germany at their own expense, even though this was covered in the case of employees by appropriating their hard-won savings. In its issue of July 22, 1921, *Stead's Review,* published in Australia, described the "refined cruelty" with which the Germans were robbed of their property and driven out of the country.

Writing of this amazing act of folly, a Melbourne correspondent of the *Manchester Guardian* wrote of the new managers (August 2, 1921):

> "They knew nothing about coconut growing, and less about the handling of natives. The inevitable has happened. The best of the native workers, who had been long on these plantations, refused to renew their contracts, preferring to go back to their own villages and await developments. The German 'boss' they had known for years - they had no confidence whatever in the young Australian 'boss' who had superseded him. Thus it has come about that the plantations are rapidly deteriorating, and at the same time the Expropriation Board is confronted with an acute shortage of labour.
>
> "The proper thing to have done was for the Australian Government to have made some arrangement to retain the experienced German planters in New Guinea. Instead, in its eagerness to obtain valuable plantations for nothing, it has driven forth the men who not only made them valuable, but could maintain their productivity.... Instead of adopting a sane policy of this kind, the Government has seized the property of all Germans, and is carrying out a policy which must soon ruin the entire colony."

A contributor to the *Westminster Gazette* (October 20, 1921) wrote strongly to the same effect. It was no better with the officials sent to administer the colony. So inexperienced were they that the German planters had to be asked for suggestions as to how the work should be carried on. In an article contributed from Raboul to the Empire Number of *The Times* of October, 1924, a correspondent states that the Australian Government had so far failed to fill the gap caused by the replacement of the Germans. He writes:

> "But the big problem still remains. Australia has to render a strict account of her stewardship in New Guinea. Her well-meant efforts to throw out the German capitalists have scarcely resulted in the development of the country; her success in handling a black race that is a shade in advance of her own primitive aborigines is still to be proved."

That is putting the case mildly from the standpoint of a friend; for the hard facts are deplorable in the extreme. It will suffice to cite the report of Mr. Ellis, a special correspondent sent to German New Guinea in 1923 on behalf of the *Sydney Daily Telegraph*. He supported his statements by numerous photographs of the plantations and cultivated territories, which were found to be neglected to an incredible degree. Everything which German industry had accomplished had been lost to civilization. Some of the unhappy German planters, whose land had been illegally taken from them by a breach of faith, were still in the colony, living in hopes that their eviction and the confiscation of their property, against which they appealed long ago, might yet be revoked. Meanwhile, they were compelled to look helplessly on while the land which during years and even decades of patient labour they had wrung from the tropical bush, suffering untold hardships and often falling a prey to disease, was being allowed to fall into decay as a result of unspeakable maladministration.

The official treatment of the natives is no better. According to the same correspondent the administration of justice is attended with various abuses, so that, as he says, "no words could be too strong to condemn the system as it stands." In that year the situation was so desperate that an expert British colonial official had to be appointed to investigate it, and in July, 1924, the Australian Government promised a Royal Commission on the subject if the report of the investigation made it advisable. In this connexion *The Times* of July 3, 1925, reporting on the action of the Mandates Commission of the League of Nations, stated in regard to New Guinea:

> "A special report has been drawn up over and above the official annual survey. The local authorities, being fully aware of their own embarrassments, themselves invited an outside opinion, and a British imperial administrator of standing and experience was sent, who has had some frank criticisms to make."

Only lack of space prevents me from enlarging further upon the results of the Mandate administration in the German colonies. The reader, however, may be referred to my book, published in 1922, *The German Colonies under the Mandates,*[15] in which much more is said on the subject in the light of the material then to hand. I wrote therein as follows upon the result of the investigations which yielded this material:

> "This result is absolutely annihilating for the majority of the colonies and the Mandatories. The Mandates have proved to be a great failure. Present conditions in these countries are in every respect infinitely worse than they were when the Germans were in possession. The German colonies are now in decay, economically and culturally. The most evil consequences for the natives arise from the collapse of the Mandatories in the matter of combating epidemics and in general health measures. The natives are absolutely dissatisfied with Mandate government."

This verdict was quite justified at that time. It cannot be maintained equally to-day for all those territories, because in the meantime some economic progress has been made. But even in those mandated territories where the greatest development has taken place it is only now that the pre-war conditions have been even approximately reached in economic affairs, while the humanitarian institutions - especially those relating to sanitation and education - are still far behind our standard.

Washing rubber, German East Africa

Rubber drying house, German East Africa

Native carpenters at work in a mission workshop, German East Africa

Printing office with native assistants, German East Africa

10

What the Natives Really Want

In the covering Note to the Treaty of Versailles the assertion is made that the Allies had had an opportunity of convincing themselves that the native populations of the German colonies had vigorously opposed the idea of being again placed under the old dominion. This assertion must be disputed. Strictly speaking it is incorrect to say that the Allied Governments or their delegates to the Peace Conference had "an opportunity of convincing themselves" one way or the other. How many of the men who signed the treaty ever entered a single German colony or had made any independent study of German colonization? What they did was to instruct their agents and proxies to prepare an indictment showing German administration in the worst possible light, and the result was accepted as justifying a foregone decision.

Several of the Allied Powers had determined from the first to annex Germany's oversea territories, and all that followed in the way of justifying that step was after-thought and pretence. Not only do Germans say this: it has been said times without number by the spokesmen of disinterested neutral nations, and even in England and France many voices have from the first been raised to the same effect. Still more untenable is the assertion that the natives of the German colonies protested against being restored to German administration. *Far from this, the behaviour of the natives, both in the war and after the war, shows plainly that they would infinitely prefer the continuance of German dominion to the dominion of the foreign Mandatories.*

I have already demonstrated that the German colonies were divided among the Powers interested with no thought or regard whatever for the wishes of the natives, who were shared out like coin or counters, their tribal unity being broken up with callous indifference both to their traditional attachments and their economic interests. Mr. Lloyd George, in speeches made at Glasgow on June 26, 1917, in the House of Commons on December 20, 1917, and to the Labour Party leaders on January 5, 1918, had promised that the fate of the natives in the German colonies should not be decided without their consent. How was that pledge kept? Some sort of inquiry as to the attitude of the natives in the colonies occupied by British troops was made by or through Government officials - the agents of the very men who had already decided the fate of the colonies, and the answers received were laid before Parliament in November, 1918, in the form of a Blue Book.[1]

The result of the inquiry was from the British point of view disappointing, and it appears in a still worse light when we consider

(1) That the purpose of the inquiry was to furnish a justification for the seizure of German colonial property by the British;

(2) That British troops had captured the territory in question by force of arms and were in complete occupation; and

(3) That the subjects of the inquiry were natives, who notoriously are given to currying favour with their patrons and easily yield to persuasion and the pressure of the moment.

The report disclosed the following facts:

(1) The result of the inquiry in **German East Africa** was absolutely unfavourable to England. The British Administrator himself expressly drew attention in his report to the fact that it was an error to suppose that the natives ever since the outbreak of war had yearned for liberation from their German rulers. He said that it would be injudicious to make

open and general inquiry of the natives as to whether they preferred British or German rule, since this procedure at the existing juncture would arouse suspicion and would exercise an unsettling effect. He further declared himself to be opposed to the application of European theories of "self-determination" to the uncivilized natives of Africa, and said he thought that such application could be seriously suggested only by those whose acquaintance with the native mind was of the slightest.

(2) In the **Cameroons, Togoland, and German South-West Africa** the officials appointed for the purpose succeeded in collecting a number of declarations of chiefs who wished - or professed to wish - that British rule should be upheld, and German dominion should not be reinstated. To what degree these utterances can be regarded as representing the actual feelings of the chiefs, still less how far they represent the opinions of the inhabitants of their villages or districts, it is impossible to ascertain. But everyone who has had anything to do with African negroes knows how little importance can be attached to such opinions, extorted as they were from natives by the representatives of a Power whose troops had occupied the land in time of war. One of these officials, who had been travelling in the Cameroons in order to collect the desired evidence, remarks of his own accord:

> "It is more than probable that many people will be sceptical of the value of these statements taken *ex parte* by a man patriotically, if not personally, concerned in the purport conveyed by them."

The official in question, who uttered such unquestionably sound common sense, nevertheless proceeded to claim entire sincerity for the protestations of the chiefs in his district. No doubt he acted in good faith in so doing, but the fact is incontestible that any representative of another Power which succeeded in taking these territories from the British by force of arms would at once be able to collect as much evidence as he wanted in his own country's favour and against that of the country dispossessed. Considering the circumstances in which the inquiries were made in the three colonies and the actual results obtained, the British had very little reason for satisfaction or encouragement; and the obvious explanation is that the natives in reality were at heart attached to German rule, believed that it would be reinstated, and were therefore only with difficulty brought to assent to a declaration such as their new masters wished to obtain from them.

(3) In the South Seas the results in **German New Guinea** were quite negative. The Australian Administrator there reported that in consequence of the isolation of the natives in many small tribes, living on various islands and with different dialects, it was impossible to acquire any reliable indication of their wishes with regard to the future government of the colony. Such a negative statement means much more than it says. With regard to **Samoa,** the answer seems at first sight somewhat dubious. The Governor-General of New Zealand reported on January 10, 1918, that he had no doubt that the decision would be in favour of England if the wishes of the natives were to be ascertained. Only the *Faipules* (chiefs), however, would be empowered to transmit this decision: for a popular vote would be contrary to all Samoan custom. It was, however, to be anticipated that in such a case the money and influence of the Germans still in Samoa would be brought to bear to the utmost in order to wean the Samoans away from the English cause!

Only after another telegram from London did the Administrator cable to the effect that the Samoan chiefs had shown themselves "practically" unanimous in their desire to remain under British rule. The report of the Administrator, received later, shows that he had sought out individual chiefs. These chiefs held a meeting in the Toeaina Club of Samoa (according to the report a politico-commercial club frequented by the leading chiefs of all Samoan districts) and passed a resolution, subsequently communicated to the Administrator, that the meeting was unanimous in the desire that Samoa should remain under British rule. This club resolution is in remarkable contradiction to the petition later directed by the Samoan Council, *the appointed representative body of the Samoan people,* to the King of England, begging him to set aside the New Zealand mandatory administration. To this I shall return later. In the meantime, Mr. Massey, the Premier of New Zealand, in a speech made at the British imperial Conference in London (October 2, 1923), in which he spoke of the presumptive contentment of the Samoans, declared: "At first the native population of Samoa was somewhat doubtful as to whether the change (in the government) would be to its advantage."[2] This shows plainly enough how little value can be placed upon the club declaration obtained by unknown means from the Samoan chiefs by the Administrator.

It is not too much to say that no one with the slightest knowledge of native habits of mind, or even of the value of evidence, would attach importance to the opinions obtained in the circumstances described. There are English publicists - as one would expect - who from the first ridiculed the so-called investigation as childish in method and worthless in results, and relegated it to the limbo to which journalistic "stunts" belong.

Criticizing in the British House of Commons on February 19, 1925, the handing over to Italy of British territory in East Africa without consulting the natives,[3] Sir R. Hamilton, a Liberal member, said "he agreed that attempts to consult the natives of areas in Africa as to whether they wished to be handed over from one Power to another were apt to be somewhat illusory." But this is true without any reservation whatever, and it applied to all undeveloped native populations, whether African or not. So the blessed principle of "self-determination" was again given the go-by.

In order to divine faithfully what were the real desires of the native population of the German colonies, it is necessary to bear in mind their behaviour during the war. It has already been mentioned that with scarcely an exception the natives in all the German colonies remained true and loyal to their masters during the war. It is important to consider what this loyalty really implied. Nowhere were there more than small bodies of Protectorate or police troops - just enough to maintain order and quiet in the country during time of peace. Soon after the outbreak of war, enemy troops broke into the colonies, in every case outnumbering considerably the few German troops, and infinitely better equipped. Is it not plain as day that these troops would have been hailed as deliverers, and that their appearance would have given the signal for a universal rising, or at least for great local revolts, if the natives had really wished to free themselves from German rule? Would not the blacks, had they been forcibly subjugated by a brutal tyranny, have seized this golden opportunity to throw off the yoke? Would not the coloured troops themselves have mutinied, if German rule had been the hated one it has maliciously been pictured? For in all colonies, except German South-West Africa, these troops were drawn from the colony in which they were stationed.

The fact is that the Germans experienced no native revolts at all during the war, whereas the British had a rising in British Nyasaland and the Portuguese one in Mozambique. The Germans also had no mutinies, while the British in the first year of war were forced to contend with a mutiny of Sikhs in India. This is the more surprising when one remembers that the Germans, totally cut off from home supplies, and insufficiently furnished with troops and war material, were incomparably worse off in their colonies than their enemies.

These facts alone are the best proof that the natives did not hate German rule. But still stronger testimony can be cited. This is the positive proof supplied by the aid given to the Germans by the natives during the war under the most arduous conditions. I call special attention to German East Africa, partly because in this great colony more than in any of the others it would have been quite impossible for the Germans to maintain their position but for the unflagging assistance of the brave and loyal blacks, partly because in my position as Governor before and during the war I am personally able to vouch for all the statements made.

It is beyond doubt that the defence of the colony for so long a time was only made possible through the untiring devotion of the natives. The faithful co-operation of the black carriers was absolutely indispensable to the marching troops for the supply of food, for fresh stores of munition, etc. Marches far into solitary regions, lasting weeks or even months, were necessary in order to fetch food and other necessaries. Many thousands, even tens of thousands, of carriers were always on the move in various parts of the colony. There were so few Europeans that very often the caravans had only black overseers. This was not all. Since there was no possibility of receiving new supplies from oversea, it was necessary for the colonists themselves to manufacture all the needful articles which had hitherto been imported. Hides were treated, leather tanned, shoes made, hand-spinning and weaving introduced on a large scale, in order to replenish the stocks of clothing. Quinine, wax candles, soap, substitutes for benzine and petroleum, and many other substitutes were manufactured. Bank-notes were made and coins were struck from gold and brass. All these things were possible only with the help of masses of natives, who were drilled to wonderful efficiency in their new tasks under German leadership.

Is it possible that a native workman could be brought to learn such perfectly unfamiliar tasks if he were possessed with the one thought of breaking away from a hated master? The idea is ludicrous. There were only a few thousand Germans, scattered in the midst of nearly eight million blacks, and threatened on all sides by strong bodies of enemy troops. It is obvious that no force which this minority could exercise, but only the sentiments of genuine fidelity and devotion, could have produced these results. Not only is the stand taken by the native population during the war a superb proof of their loyalty to the German Government, however, but it is also a vindication of the methods used by the Germans in governing them.

The strongest proof of devotion was that given by the Askari and carriers, who towards the close of the war left the colony with us, marching into Portuguese territory and later into Rhodesia. They left their homes, their relations, and their huts, and followed the Germans into a precarious future, enduring terrible hardships, privation, and danger. Even our enemies have not dared to declare that these warriors were actuated in this behaviour by the wish to subject themselves to another rule. They have found a new prevarication. They say that the Askari were a peculiarly privileged class! This is not true, but even if it were it does not explain why so many of the carriers endured with us to the end. They at least were certainly not a specially privileged class!

The simple truth is that the natives, satisfied, and more than satisfied, with German sovereignty, desired nothing better than its continuance. Can it surprise anyone capable of manly and generous feelings that the German nation will never forget such fidelity, or renounce the right to return to the territory in which it was shown, whatever formal declarations to the contrary were exacted in its name under pressure of military menace, suffering, and starvation? *Would Englishmen or Americans be guilty of such poltroonery, and if not, why should others?*

After the war the native populations of the German colonies were, under the Mandate system, "bartered about from sovereignty to sovereignty as if they were mere chattels and pawns in a game," in total disregard of President Wilson's Point 5, supposed to be a foundation-stone of the Peace, and also of Point 2 as originally formulated in his speech in Congress on February 11, 1918, viz.: "There shall be no annexations, no contributions, no punitive damages." After the failure of the mock inquiry of 1918, no further attempt was made to fulfil Mr. Lloyd George's pledges that the native population should be really consulted.

In the meantime and subsequently native protests issued from various colonies, including several from the Cameroons and Togoland, against their transference from German rule.[4] The protests against the surrender of large tracts of both colonies to France were particularly vigorous.[5] The strongest protest of all was that already mentioned, the petition sent by the Samoan Council to the King of England in June, 1921.[6] In the course of this impressive statement the united chiefs of Samoa "begged to be free from the control of the New Zealand Government on account of their continually increasing discontent with its rule." It is true that the appeal does not explicitly ask that Samoa might be given back to Germany, for the Samoans, who are schooled in politics, may not have considered this a practical possibility. Assuming that the new territorial status could not be changed, they simply begged to be put directly under the Colonial Office in London. But the content of the petition, none the less, allows it to be clearly seen that the Samoans were thoroughly content under German rule and failed to appreciate the hypocritical pretence that the annexations were enforced in the name of the high-sounding doctrine of "self-determination" and "in the interests of the little nations."

The small community of the Samoan people is the only group of inhabitants of the German colonies which is sufficiently organized politically to be in a position to express its wishes in a united manner calculated to make a strong public impression. Such united protests are unthinkable in the other colonies, where the natives are on a lower plane of civilization and divided into numerous petty tribes. Nevertheless, sufficient evidence comes from all the former colonies that the natives are weary of Mandate administration and long for the return of the Germans. Could it, indeed, be otherwise? All the colonial territories which were blossoming under German rule are now being economically ruined. The earning capacity of the natives has been lowered, but taxes and tribute have not been minimized, but, on the contrary, have been increased in some colonies. The days of German rule appear to the natives, in these times of growing poverty and economic decay, as "the good old times," the return of which is ardently desired. The blacks also miss the many cultural advantages formerly offered them by the Germans. All this is abundantly evident from many touching individual letters which natives from the various colonies have addressed to their former employers, to missionaries, and others.

Various signs and occurrences in the colonies themselves have demonstrated the existence of this feeling. Wherever Germans appear in the Mandate regions they are at once greeted with every manifestation of joy, and their presence is heralded as a sign that the happier days of German rule will return. Such was the case when the first German steamers appeared again in colonial harbours. They were greeted by crowds of many thousands of enthusiastic natives. This was also the case on the arrival of individuals who had been associated with the work of civilization among the natives. It may be sufficient to call attention to the reception accorded to the first three German missionaries (from the North German Missionary Society of Bremen) who returned in 1923 to the scene of their former labours in Togoland. Their journey through the Eweland and their arrival at the mission-station formed one long triumphal progress. Wherever they came, crowds of natives poured from all directions; whole villages turned out to welcome them; they had to pass under triumphal arches amid frantic cheering and waving of flags; and the chief of Apafu met the travellers with music. "There are our own again!" was the cry that rang joyously from all sides.[7]

These are a few facts symptomatic of the real as opposed to the make-believe feelings and wishes of the natives. The prevailing sentiment everywhere is totally unfavourable to Mandate rule, under which the natives have neither the economic nor the cultural advantages which German rule gave them in the past and can alone give them in the future. If a genuine, uninfluenced, and impartial plebiscite could be taken, Germany would need to have no fear as to the result of the native vote.

11

The Future - the Way of Peace

Little remains of my task except to gather up the loose threads of my narrative and to draw conclusions. As a German suffering from an intolerable sense of wrong, and that all the more keenly because of the years of arduous labour directly given to the welfare of the natives of our colonies as well as to the interests of our country, I have written strongly yet, I believe, moderately - probably far more moderately than most of my readers would have written in the same circumstances. I would urge our late antagonists to remember that they have no monopoly of patriotism, pride of country and race, and attachment to colonial settlements and enterprises created by untold sacrifice both of blood and treasure. I would ask them also: "Do you want our co-operation in the tasks of civilization, or do you prefer that we should seek our own ways of carrying on those tasks without regard for you? Do you want us to be co-workers with you for the maintenance of peace in the world, or would you rather perpetuate the rancours and resentments caused by the war and prolonged even more acutely by the peace?" It is for you, not for us, to choose and decide.

The German people urgently need and ardently desire peace - not temporary but permanent peace; but such a peace must be compatible with national honour, or it will be unreal, illusory, and will not endure. What their honour calls for, and will compel them to claim until the need for so doing exists no longer, is that in this matter of the colonies the Powers now in possession of our oversea territories will observe faithfully and honourably the conditions of peace as proposed to us by the American Government, endorsed by its Allies, and thereafter accepted by Germany prior to her relinquishment of the late struggle. The Allies have failed to keep their word, and have set at naught the basis of peace originally agreed upon. I have shown in the foregoing pages how, ignoring President Wilson's Point 5, they divided the German colonies among themselves, without any consideration either for us as a nation or for the interests of the natives, and solely from the point of view of *Macht-Politik*[1] and partly in accordance with secret treaties concluded during the war.

Later they put forward moral and altruistic reasons for the seizure and appropriation of these territories, and set up the baseless and ludicrous thesis that Germany had proved herself incapable and unworthy of colonization, and had wickedly planned to establish naval bases from which to threaten the security of other nations. All these untrue and untenable charges have been disproved, and disproved without difficulty. It must be clear to the minds of all unprejudiced persons that the objectives of Germany's colonial policy were confined to the economic development of her Protectorates and to the preservation and cultural advancement of the natives.

Furthermore, it has been made equally clear that no military or naval bases have been established in the colonies, and that such were not even planned, and also that only small bodies of police troops were maintained at the various stations. Nor can it be denied that the war was carried into the colonies, not by Germany, but by her enemies, and that some of her territories were invaded by them in direct violation both of the spirit and the letter of the Congo Act. It is also manifest that the militarization of German colonies has been accomplished not while these colonies were in the hands of their rightful owners, the Germans, but only since they have been under the mandate of the French.

The accusations levelled against the German colonial administration on the score of misgovernment, of cruel oppression of the natives, of "wanton requisitions," of an unfair code of laws, and of depopulation due to forced labour, have similarly been exposed as mere propagandist fictions. It has been conceded that abuses and mistakes occurred in the German as they have done in all other colonies and still do in some, and that individual whites at times egregiously overrode the rights of individual blacks, and committed acts unworthy of their country; though here, again, the colonial record of other Powers is not free from the same reproach. At the worst, however, these cases of wrong-doing were sporadic, and the German Government was honestly striving in every way to prevent them.

Sufficient evidence has also been furnished to prove how extensive and efficacious were the cultural achievements of Germany in her colonies, especially in relation to the welfare of her black charges, and that the administration of the Mandates has not been able even to preserve the work or maintain the standards which Germany had created, much less improve upon them. It is also clear that the natives at no time desired the abolition of the German rule, but that, on the contrary, they have longed for the return of the Germans, after experiencing all the rigours and disadvantages incidental to Mandate government.

What conclusions follow from these facts? What inference must be drawn after this exposure of so much deliberate mis-statement and misrepresentation? Surely it is abundantly evident that a great and indefensible wrong has been committed against the German people in robbing them of their colonial possessions; and not only against the German people, but against the whole white race, and no less against the black race to whose improvement and elevation Germany had for a generation so sincerely, assiduously, and successfully devoted herself. The spurious reasons advanced for the seizure of Germany's colonies, though they may hitherto have been deemed conclusive by the indifferent, the prejudiced, and the uninformed, cannot stand serious examination; brought into contact with the truth, they are seen to be hollow, unsubstantial fictions, and with their exposure falls to the ground the entire structure of calumny and defamation in which the annexationist

Powers have hitherto succeeded in concealing the real motives of their illegal action.

I am not without hope of carrying with me no small section of the fair-minded among my readers, even those who have lately been the enemies of my country, in the conclusion that Germany has an incontrovertible right to claim the return of her colonies - to claim and receive them. Whether, when the question is practically faced - as faced it assuredly will be sooner or later - the claim should or will be pressed with literal exactitude may be a matter for careful consideration; but though many Germans might now be disposed to favour a policy of compromises and readjustments, always within measure, it would show a lack of candour not to avow the conviction that the longer the settlement of this question is delayed the more difficult must be the task of conciliating divergent views and interests. No menace should be read into these words, for none is intended. What is said is no more than an expression of political wisdom and common sense, and the man or woman who does not recognize this has yet to learn the elements of statesmanship.

The claim that Germany shall be reinstated in the ranks of colonizing Powers, with a status equal to that which she won for herself by untold exertions and sacrifices during a struggle lasting over thirty years, is not merely one that concerns the German people. It concerns all nations engaged in colonization; indeed, it concerns all humanity and civilization at large. For the issue involved is plainly this - whether a whole continent and an entire race are to suffer from the fact that the German colonies have been handed over to nations already satiated with such possessions and who, burdened with immense and formidable colonial problems, have neither the inclination nor the necessary forces to devote themselves to the great constructive tasks which modern colonization implies. Shall the unhappy native people of our Protectorates continue to be exposed to decimation by plagues and diseases with which the British, French, and Belgians have shown inability to cope adequately alone? Shall a great, highly cultured, and efficient nation like the Germans, a nation which, by the testimony of the whole world, has performed such wonders in the domain of science, medicine, hygiene, education, and industry, which has sent forth into the dark places of the earth so many skilled, conscientious, and self-sacrificing physicians, missionaries, and teachers, be excluded from this great cultural work, for which it is so remarkably fitted? To answer this question is to deny it, and to deny it with the utmost possible emphasis.

If Europe remains sick under the curse of the calumnies and brute force embodied in the Treaty of Versailles, Africa will remain sick and undeveloped for the same reason. This interaction is inherent in the operation of an inexorable moral law, which neither nations nor Governments, which are nations in miniature, can violate without harming all mankind. Untruth has triumphed for a time, and its results are seen in a Europe that is rotting and in an Africa that has gone backward in many ways. But the destruction of cultural values and the obstruction of progress are acts which will assuredly avenge themselves upon those who have either committed, approved, or still persist in tolerating them.

Even now this is what is actually taking place, as all who have eyes to see, minds to understand, and human hearts to feel can perceive for themselves. The men, whoever they were, who in their hatred, cupidity, and blindness wrecked the prestige of the white man in Africa by unloosing the dogs of war in the sight of undeveloped peoples, peoples gifted, however, with keen instincts and powers of observation, will yet bitterly rue the day that saw the perpetration of this unexampled blunder and crime against humanity and civilization. The wise of all nations, whether neutral or combatant, have known this from the beginning, and have feared exceedingly because they knew it. Happily there are signs that the truth is beginning to dawn upon others, whose minds have returned to a normal temper and are no longer closed to the influences of reflection and reason.

But, finally, while Germany claims the opportunity and the right to take her part again permanently in the civilizing mission of the white races, now so much more urgent than ever before owing to the ground lost for the reasons just stated, she makes this claim also for her own sake and in the interest of her own national development and progress. Falsehood may for a time resist, but it cannot successfully overcome, the inexorable demands of Truth and Justice, nor thwart the will to live and the right to grow and prosper of a great, cultured, industrious, and peace-loving people.

12

Notes

Introduction

1. Such were the fifth article of the Protocol signed at St. Petersburg on April 4, 1826, of the conferences between the British and Russian plenipotentiaries relative to the mediation of Great Britain between Turkey and Greece; the fifth article of the Treaty of July 6, 1827, for the pacification of Greece, concluded between Great Britain, France, and Russia; the third Protocol of the Conferences of 1840 respecting the pacification of the Levant, between Great Britain, Austria, Prussia, Russia, and Turkey; the fourth article of the Convention of April 10, 1854, between Great Britain and France preliminary to the Crimean War; the second Protocol of the conferences of 1860 on the pacification of Syria, between Great Britain, France, Prussia, Russia, and Turkey; and the agreement of September 21, 1880, by which, on the proposal of Lord Granville, France, Italy, Germany, Austria-Hungary, and Russia, with Great Britain, "in order to prove anew the entire disinterestedness with which they pursue the execution of all the stipulations of the Treaty of Berlin, (engage) not to seek in any arrangements which may be come to in consequence of their concerted action for the execution of the said Treaty in regard to the Montenegrin question, and eventually the Greek question, any acquisition of territory, any exclusive influence,

or any commercial advantages for their subjects which those of every other nation may not equally obtain."

2. Lord Morley's *Autobiography,* vol. i, pp. 69-70.

3. *The Peace Negociations,* p. 345.

4. I mention only two instances which came to my own knowledge in the course of a conversation with President Wilson on April 17, 1919. One was the ludicrous statement contained in a Memorandum circulated amongst his colleagues by M. Clemenceau, in support of the French demand for the outright annexation of the Saar Valley, that there were 150,000 inhabitants of French nationality (that is, one-fifth of the total population) in that region, the fact being that there were not a hundred (though since the French occupation the number has grown to about 12,000); and the other was the statement made in justification of the Polish claim to the full absorption of Danzig in the new Polish State, that in the past the German Government had deliberately obstructed the prosperity of the port, the fact being precisely the reverse. Both of these misapprehensions I had the opportunity of correcting and, I hope, of removing.

5. *The Evolution of Modern Germany.*

6. I refer here to the testimony borne by Mr. E. Bevan in the Introduction to *The German Empire of Central Africa* (1918): " It is fair to do justice to the movement for considerate treatment of the native peoples which had no doubt made *some way* in Germany before the war, and had found support in missionary, as well as in Social-Democratic circles." But these words state only partially and grudgingly a well-attested fact. The movement referred to was by no means confined to the Socialist Party in the Diet, and it had made great headway in practical administration, even before the tenure of the Colonial Secretaryship by Dr. Dernburg (1906 - 1910), who, with the assistance of our Colonial Office, made visits of study and comparison to British colonies. Dr. Schnee gives evidence on this point in the later pages.

7. *Foreign Office Miscellaneous Series,* 1894, No. 346 (C 7582-7), p. 54.

8. *The Partition of Africa* (1893), p. 259.

9. Great Britain, France, Holland, Belgium, Italy, Spain, and Portugal. Since Denmark in 1916 sold her West Indian (now Virgin) Islands to the United States only Greenland remains to her as a dependency.

10. Of a population estimated in 1921 at 39¼ millions, 1½ millions were foreigners. According to the Paris correspondent of *The Times*, the number of foreigners in France is now (November, 1925) over three millions.

11. In *Pan-Germanism* (1913), by Mr. R. G. Usher, an American historian, a work warmly welcomed in this country during the war, there occurs the following passage which deserves thought: "The financial operations known as peaceful penetration are not exactly what we have been accustomed to consider methods of violent conquest, but by such means large numbers of the inhabitants of the smaller countries have just as certainly lost their land and the products of their labour as if an army had destroyed them. There is, perhaps, a nice discrimination to be drawn by some logicians between taking a man's property away from him or stealing a nation's independence by means of an army and by means of high finance; but if the individual or the nation suffers the same loss from both processes, and if the intent is essentially the same, it is difficult to see where the ethical grounds supporting them differ" (p. 246). These words apply far less to Germany than to some other countries.

12. Cf. Mr. E. Bevan, in his Introduction to *The German Empire of Central Africa:* "It is fair to remember that Dr. Solf's own record as a colonial administrator is a high one in the matter of justice and solicitude for the welfare of the native peoples" (February, 1918).

13. Anticipating the possible objection that in 1916 Dr. Solf had hinted at the desirability of increasing in future the number of native as well as white troops in the colonies, I would point out that he expressly stated that the object in view was that "we need not in any future war look forward to the certainty of losing our colonies over again, but rather to the possibility, at worst, of a temporary separation." Such a

measure of purely defensive militarization, if it may be so called, is sanctioned by all the mandates.

14. Many years ago Schmoller estimated the population of Germany in 1965 at 104,000,000; Hübbe-Schleiden estimated it at 150,000,000 in 1980; and Leroy-Beaulieu at 200,000,000 in the year 2000. (*Scriptorium adds, to put this into present-day perspective:* Germany has in fact suffered from a birth deficit for well over a century and the currently remaining population growth is due to the presence of many non-Germans, who tend to have larger families. In 2022 the population of Germany was in actuality only 84.3 million, with *well over one-quarter* of people currently living in Germany *being either foreign-born or having at least one immigrant parent.* The latest numbers, published by Germany's statistics agency Destatis, show that "people with migrant background" make up **27.2%** of Germany's population. [With data from worldometers.info, statista.com and dw.com])

15. *Problems of the Peace* (1917), pp. 66-70.

16. *Commonsense in Foreign Policy* (1913), pp. 40 and 49.

17. The literature on this subject is, of course, enormous and is in many languages. While writing this Introduction the striking book Les Criminels, by M. Victor Margueritte, significantly dedicated *"aux survivants et à leurs fils,"* has fallen into my hands. It can be recommended only to truth-seekers, for others will not read it. It is to have as a sequel a volume to be called *Les Victimes.* Critics the least sympathetic to Germany, upon which the punitive effects of the war have been concentrated, are to-day compelled to accept President Wilson's diagnosis of the European situation which existed in 1914, that "no single fact caused the war, but that in the last analysis the whole European system is in a deeper sense responsible for the war, with its complication of alliances and understandings, a complicated texture of intrigues and espionage that unfailingly caught the whole family of nations in its meshes" (October 20, 1916). The remarkable revelations contained in Siebert's collection of Russian diplomatic documents, translated into German with the title *Diplomatische Aktenstücke zur Geschichte der*

Ententepolitik der Vorkriegsjahre (1921), abound in proofs of the truth of Wilson's words.

18. *The German Empire, 1867-1914*, vol. ii, pp. 280-7.

How the German Colonies Were Seized

1. Cf. the President's declaration to the effect that "Having received the solemn and explicit assurance of the German Government that it unreservedly accepts the terms of peace laid down in his address to Congress of the United States on January 8, 1918, and the principles of settlement enunciated in his subsequent addresses, and particularly the address of September 27th," he agreed to take up with the other Governments the question of an Armistice, etc. Points 1 and 2, as developed in the later address, ran:

> "Impartial justice must involve no discrimination between those to whom we wish to be just and those to whom we wish to be unjust, and the equal rights of the several peoples concerned must be secured.
>
> "No special interest of any nation can be made the basis of any settlement which is not consistent with the common interest of all."

2. See Ray Stannard Baker, *Woodrow Wilson and World Settlement* (London, 1923), vol. i, chap. xv, pp. 250-75.

3. Ray Stannard Baker, *Woodrow Wilson and World Settlement* (London, 1923), vol. i, p. 225.

4. Ray Stannard Baker, *Woodrow Wilson and World Settlement* (London, 1923), vol i, pp. 253-4.

5. Cf. Secret Protocol of the Council of Four, April 22, 1919, in Baker, vol. i, p. 60.

6. Reprinted *verbatim* in Baker, vol. i, p. 61.

7. Secret Protocol of the Council of Ten, January 28, 1919, quoted in Baker, vol. i, p. 268.

8. *Le Temps,* January 30, 1919.
9. Cf. Baker, vol. i, p. 54.
10. Baker, vol. i, p. 296.
11. Robert Lansing, *The Peace Negociations* (1921), pp. 139-40. It has been calculated by colonial experts that the values represented by the German colonies exceed the costs of the war, and the potential values of the German colonies which fell to Great Britain have been estimated at thousands of millions of pounds sterling.
12. Cf. *The Peace Negociations,* p. 139.

The Myth of German "Colonial Guilt"

1. For a larger selection of such tributes from English, American, and other sources, the reader is referred to Dr. W. H. Solf's book, *Germany's Right to recover Her Colonies* (Berlin, 1919), and to *Englische Urteile über die deutsche Kolonialarbeit* ("English Verdicts on German Colonial Enterprise"), by Dr. A. Mansfeld and G. Hildebrand (Berlin, 1919).

2. *Handbooks prepared under the direction of the Historical Section of the Foreign Office* (London, 1920).

3. *Die deutsche Kolonialpolitik vor dem Gerichtshof der Welt* (Basle, 1918), p. 58.

The Alleged Militarism in the German Colonies

1. The establishment by European Powers of naval stations in Chinese territory late in the nineteenth century began with Germany's occupation of Kiao-chou in November, 1897, in partial redress for the murder of two German missionaries; China formally leased the port to Germany by treaty of January 5, 1898. Russia seized Port Arthur in December, 1897, and acquired it by a forced agreement in March following. Great Britain (who in April, 1885, seized Port Hamilton

without notice, fearing that Russia might forestall her, but abandoned it in February, 1887), obtained a lease of Wei-Hai-Wei on July 1, 1898, to last as long as Russia retained Port Arthur. Finally, France secured the Bay of Kwang-Chow-Wau in April, 1898, and in the following year the two islands in the same. - W. H. D.

2. For further evidence in disproof of these accusations against Germany, the reader is referred to *Weltpolitik vor, in und nach dem Kriege,* by the present author (1923), p. 144, etc.

3. Cf. *Deutsches Koloniallexikon,* articles on "Schutztruppen" and "Polizeitruppen," the figures being taken from official sources.

4. Cf. the article of General Verrau in *L'Œuvre* of September 22, 1923.

5. Cf. *African World,* No. 1,013, April 8, 1923.

6. See particularly the evidence given on both sides on May 2, 7, 8, and 9, 1924.

7. Cf. the official *Deutsches Kolonialblatt,* Nos. 1 - 4, of February 28, 1920, which contain the German and Belgian official documents.

8. Cf. Article on "How England prepared for the War against German South-West Africa," by Privy Councillor Dr. Hintrager, in the *Deutsch-Südwestafrikanische Zeitung* of November 4, 1918.

9. The text was published in the *Deutsch-Ostafrikanische Zeitung* (Dar-es-Salam) of November 25, 1914.

10. This information was given to me independently by Superintendent Schowalter himself, who now lives at Wittenberge, and a certified copy of his full statement, dated September 17, 1923, has been supplied to Mr. Dawson at his request.

The Allied Powers and Their "Sacred Trust"

1. Cf. Solf's essay, "Militarism and Colonial Policy," in the *Süddeutsche Monatshefte* of Munich (August, 1915).

2. *Deutsches Koloniallexikon,* vol. ii, p. 337.

3. This gratuitous and unwarranted insinuation was the more ungenerous since Mr. Lloyd George had before him Germany's thirty-five years' record to inform him better.

4. Secret Protocol of the Council of Ten of January 30, 1919, quoted in Baker, vol. i, p. 426.

5. Baker, vol. i, p. 429.

6. Secret Minutes of the Council of Four, May 5th, in Baker, vol. i, p. 430.

7. Cf. *Décret* of July 30, 1919, *Arrêts* for the Cameroons of January 1, 1920, and I*nstruction ministérielle* of February 21, 1922.

8. *Documents parlamentaires - Journal officiel de la République française,* 1924, pp. 769-813.

9. M. Delafosse, already mentioned, in *La Dépêche Coloniale et Maritime* of February 16, 1922.

The Treatment of the Natives

1. Sir Harry Johnston refers to the earnest endeavours of the Government to stamp out excesses and bring offenders to book in his book *The Colonisation of Africa* (1899), where he writes:

"Unfortunately, as amongst *some* officials of the East Africa Company, so amongst a *few* of the Government servants in the Cameroons, there were instances of great cruelties committed about three years ago, cruelties which led to a serious revolt among the negro soldiery. *Germany wisely did not hush up these affairs, but investigated them in open court and punished the guilty"* (p. 258).

Of how many colonial Powers could the words last quoted have been said then, or be said to-day?

2. Cf. *L'Humanité* of July 20, 1922, and *Le progrès civique* of October 29, 1921.

3. E. D. Morel, *Red Rubber, Great Britain and the Congo,* etc.

4. *Dawn in Darkest Africa* (1912), p. 181.

5. The manner in which British and French colonization compares with German is examined in detail in a book entitled *The Treatment of Native Populations in the Colonial Possessions of Germany and England* (2nd edition, 1919).

6. Written, he says, "with the object of showing how grave has been the injustice to 800,000 native people of Southern Rhodesia and how urgent is the need for such reparation as may still be possible."

7. Cf. *Landeszeitung für Südwestafrika,* August 25 and 27, 1923; and *Hamburger Nachrichten,* November 4, 1923.

8. The judicial regulations in French Equatorial Africa and other French colonies do not mention corporal punishment amongst the legal punishments; but in actual fact flogging is still administered both in French Equatorial and French West Africa. Cf. *How Natives are Treated in German and French Colonies* (1919), p. 12, etc.

9. *Report on the German Colonies in Africa and the South Pacific* (C 7582-7), 1894.

10. For the year 1906, p. 2298.

11. Cf. *West Africa,* February 26, 1921.

12. *Foreign Office Report* (C 8649-3) for 1897.

13. *Dépêche Coloniale et Maritime* of December 23 and 24, 1922.

14. Quoted from Secretary of State Dr. Solf's *Germany's Right to recover Her Colonies* (1919), pp. 31-2.

15. Printed in Hans Poeschel's *Die Koloniale Frage im Frieden von Versailles.*

The Question of Slavery and Forced Labour

1. *Commission permanente des Mandats: Annexes aux procès-verbaux de la 3e session tenue* 20. 7. - 10. 8. 1923, p. 263.

2. Cf. *Foreign Office Report on German Colonies for 1894,* No. 346 (C 7582-7), pp. 34-44.

3. *Ibid.,* No. 528, June, 1900.

4. *Ibid.*, No. 3519, for 1903-4.

5. *Slave-trading and Slave-owning in Abyssinia* (reprinted from the *Westminster Gazette* by the Anti-Slavery and Aborigines Protection Society [1922]).

6. The episode is dealt with in an official White Paper (Cmd. 2464) issued in London in July, 1925.

7. Forced labour of another kind has since been reported from South Africa. The *Cape Argus* of May 30, 1925, published a paragraph from Johannesburg entitled "Persecuted Bushmen," stating: "Dr. C. M. Doke, the well-known expert on native affairs, declared in a lecture at the Y.M.C.A. last night, that Kalahari Bushmen are being captured in raids and compelled to work in farmers' fields. The lecturer alleged that even to-day in Angola Bushmen were being hunted and persecuted."

8. Professor Brinckmann, "Eine Unterredung mit Pater van der Burgt," in the *Koloniale Rundschau* (1918), p. 437.

9. Cf. *Commission permanente des Mandats: Rapport sur les travaux de la troisième session de la commission présente au Conseil de la Société des Nations du 20 juillet au 10 août, 1923*, p. 2, No. 3.

10. *Commission permanente des Mandats: Annexes aus procès-verbaux de la 3e Session tenue à Genève du 20 juillet au 10 août, 1923*, p. 269.

11. *Rapport au Ministre des Colonies sur l'administration des territoires occupés du Cameroun pendant l'année 1921* (Paris, 1922).

German Rule and Mandate Rule Compared

1. See also the *Tanga Post and East Coast Advertiser* as quoted in the *Weser Zeitung* of March 29, 1921.

2. As reported in *The Times* at the time.

3. Cf. *Official Report of Parliamentary Debates*, p. 509.

4. Cf. *Report on the British Sphere of the Cameroons, Parliamentary Publications*, May, 1922, p. 62.

5. *Ibid.*, p. 68.

6. *Landeszeitung* for September 18, 1920.

7. Report of the proceedings in the *Westminster Gazette,* August 16, 1920.

8. *Rapport au ministre des Colonies sur l'administration... du Cameroun de la Conquête au 1 juillet, 1921,* p. 434.

9. *Rapport, 1921,* p. 24.

10. *L'Intransigéant,* as quoted in the *Hamburgische Korrespondenten,* August 18, 1923.

11. Cf. *Dar-es-Salam Times,* August 25, 1923.

12. *Ibid.,* April 21 and May 5,1923, and *African World,* May 26, 1923.

13. *The Times,* May 24, 1923.

14. *Gold Coast Independent,* April 24, 1923, cited by the *African World* of May 19, 1923.

15. Published by Quelle and Meyer, of Leipzig.

What the Natives Really Want

1. *Correspondence relating to the Wishes of the Natives of the German Colonies as to their future Government* (Cd. 9210).

2. Cf. *United Empire,* November, 1923, p. 649.

3. This territory consists of a large part of Jubaland, in Eastern Kenya, bordering on the Italian dependency of Somaliland, and it was given to Italy in fulfilment of an undertaking contained in the Treaty of London, concluded with Italy early in 1915. By that treaty Italy stipulated for a cession of African territory in consideration of her entering the war on the side of the Entente Powers. - W. H. D.

4. Some of these protests are reprinted in Dr. Poeschel's *The Colonial Question in the Peace of Versailles* (1920), p. 43.

5. Cf. *Le Temps,* No. 1543, dated June 29, 1920, and *West Africa* of March 5, 1921.

6. Reprinted in my pamphlet, *The German Colonies under the Mandates,* p. 83.

7. Cf. *Hamburger Nachrichten* for November 13, 1923.

The Future - the Way of Peace

1. Literally "policy of power," meaning here the assertion of the doctrine of Might before Right. - W. H. D.

For more books on this subject and many other little-known aspects of German history, please visit us at VersandbuchhandelScriptorium.com and our sister site wintersonnenwende.com !

Featured publications include:

• the German original of *German Colonization Past and Future* by **Dr. Heinrich Schnee: Die koloniale Schuldlüge.** Buchverlag der Süddeutschen Monatshefte, München © 1926.

• *Falsehood in War-Time: Containing an Assortment of Lies Circulated Throughout the Nations During the Great War.* Arthur Ponsonby, MP. London, Garland Publishing Company, 1928.

• *Die deutschen Kolonien vor, in und nach dem Weltkrieg.* Dr. Heinrich Schnee. Verlag von Quelle & Meyer in Leipzig © 1935.

• *Was Deutschland an seinen Kolonien verlor.* Dr. Arthur Dix. Verlag der Werbestelle "Wieder Kolonien", Berlin SW 48, Wilhelmstr. 29, ©1926[?].

• *Unsere großen Afrikaner: Das Leben deutscher Entdecker und Kolonialpioniere.* Ewald Banse. Haude & Spenersche Verlagsbuchhandlung Max Paschke, Berlin © 1942.

More titles are being added regularly in German and English.

www.ingramcontent.com/pod-product-compliance
Lightning Source LLC
Chambersburg PA
CBHW050345120526
44590CB00015B/1567